A HISTORY OF
GOLF

The Origins of Golf

Development of the Game

Spreading the Gospel of Golf

The Great Triumvirate

The Ladies' Game

The Big Three

The Famous Five

Ten Greatest Golf Courses

A HISTORY OF

GOLF

This new and revised edition first published in the UK in 2004
by Green Umbrella exclusively for
Sutton Publishing · Phoenix Mill · Thrupp · Stroud · Gloucestershire · GL5 2BU

First published in the UK in 2003

British Library Cataloguing in Publication Data
A catalogue record for this book is available from the British Library

Printed and bound in Hong Kong

ISBN 0 7509 3952 4

The Ultimate Amateur

An American Triumvirate

21st Century Golf

Greatest Ever Ryder Cup Teams

A HISTORY OF

GOLF

TABLE OF CONTENTS

BERNARD GALLACHER

FOREWORD

Trying to condense several centuries of golf history into a single volume is no easy task, but this book is tangible proof that it can be done. When I read the manuscript for the first time, I was impressed with its breadth of content.

Bernard Gallacher

Bernard Gallacher

This book's strengths lie in several key areas. Crucially, it chronicles the defining moments in the way the game of golf has evolved through the centuries. From ancient documents and paintings we are able to put a finger on the moments in time when golf came into being. From those early reference points, this book gives us a guided tour through history, bringing us right up to the 21st century.

In each moment of time we are introduced to the great players, men and women, who to many golf fans might be known only in old black-and-white photographs. Old Tom Morris, Harry Vardon, James Braid, Walter Hagen, Bobby Jones, Ben Hogan, Babe Zaharias, Henry Cotton and Sam Snead; those legendary golfers are all no longer with us, but this book brings them and many of their contemporaries to life with insightful stories of their achievements and how they played the game. With such words comes a greater appreciation of their skills and their contribution to the game. The great players of the modern era are accorded similar treatment.

Woven like thread into these stories is a marvellous attention to detail, and some wonderful little anecdotes, which together help define each era. The passages which chart the evolution of golf equipment are particularly fascinating.

On a personal note, having played in eight Ryder Cups and been captain three times, it was fun for me to sit down and choose my all-time, ultimate European dream team. I'd have certainly enjoyed leading my captain's dozen into competition against the United States. Any one of the 10 great golf courses of the world featured in this book would have been a fitting venue.

The great Bobby Jones, arguably the finest player of all time, once described the Old Course at St Andrews in such a way as to say that the more he played it, the more he got to like it, and so the more he wanted to learn about it. I find that golf itself is self-fulfilling in much the same way. The more we know of its history and its wonderful characters, the more we can appreciate the game.

This book certainly succeeded in enhancing my knowledge of golf and I enjoyed it immensely. I'm sure you will do, too.

The Origins of Golf

Chapter ONE

The Origins of Golf

Where it began, no one knows. The origin is lost in the mists of time.

It might have been on a country road in Normandy, or in an alley near the Roman forum. It might have been in sand dunes above the North Sea, or on a hillside overlooking Peking. It might have been in a field in Flanders or a courtyard in London or on the frozen surface of a Dutch canal.

No one can say precisely where or when the game of golf was born, but one thing is certain, no other form of recreation has transfixed its practitioners with such engaging appeal.

Today, in the beginnings of the 21st century, hardly a country in the civilised world remains untouched by the glorious epidemic that is golf. Its lure is difficult to define, impossible to exaggerate – an obsession that can begin at any age and last a lifetime.

The elemental appeal of golf stems from one of man's primal instincts: the urge to strike an object with a stick. Indeed, a reasonable skill in club-swinging surely was key to the survival of the caveman. It's not hard to envisage homo erectus hefting a sturdy tree limb to swat at stones or bones or whatever came into his path. In this sense, the notion – or at least the motion – of golf is older than civilisation itself. Fundamentally, golf was not invented; it was born within us.

But it was civilisation that gave the game its spin. Depending on whom we choose to believe, the first primeval golf shots were struck somewhere between 2,000 and 600 years ago. The earliest possible ancestor dates to the Roman Empire. It seems that the Roman soldiers were enthusiastic sportsmen, and one of the ways they kept in fighting trim was by playing paganica, a game in which they swatted at a feather-stuffed ball with curved sticks.

But all evidence suggests that this was a team sport, and that the ball the troops were striking was moving, not still. Thus, if paganica was the forerunner of a modern game, it was more likely hockey than golf.

Illustrated scrolls from the early Ming Dynasty (mid-to-late 1300s) depict something called suigan, described as "a game in which you hit a ball with a stick while walking". At least one scholar has suggested that the silk traders of the late Middle Ages might have exported this or a similar game to Europe, where it was spun and refined into golf.

A stained-glass window in Gloucester Cathedral, dating from the mid-14th century, shows a figure wielding a stick in the middle of a distinctly golf-like backswing. Was this golf? Possibly. But it might also have been another stick-and-ball game, with the

• Opposite
Golfers outside the clubhouse at St Andrews – attending the Open Championship, 1860.

• Above
Scrolls from the Ming Dynasty suggest the Chinese may have been the first golfers.

• Below
A golf-like swing, circa 1350, from a window at Gloucester Cathedral.

exotic name cambuca, which was known to be played in England at the time.

Across the Channel the French had taken to a rather genteel courtyard game called Jeu de mail. Originally developed in Italy, it was a curious blend of billiards, croquet, and miniature golf, played with long-handled mallets and large wooden balls within a well-defined area. The object was to hit the ball through one or more iron hoops, using the fewest possible strokes.

Jeu de mail caught on briefly in England where it became the rage of the ruling class under the name 'pall mall'. It was first played in London on the street with the same name, which now runs between Buckingham Palace and Piccadilly Circus. Back in 1629, King Charles I was an avid pall maller, and the court of St James included an impressive 1,000-yard-long area for royal play.

By the 18th century, however, this game had played out, except in southern France where a more expansive version saw the Basques hitting over hill and dale to targets such as the sides of barns and pasture gates. Shades of golf there, for sure.

Meanwhile, in Belgium they were hooked on chole, a game with a delightfully spiteful quality. It was played cross country, usually in teams, with the players wielding heavy iron clubs to propel an egg-shaped wooden ball distances of up to 400 yards. A target – a church door, a tree, almost anything – was established, sometimes as much as a mile away, and then the two teams bid on the number of shots needed to hit it. The low-bidding team led off by taking three strokes toward the target. Then the opponents, known as decholeurs, were allowed one stroke to send the ball into the nastiest possible trouble. Thereafter, the offence resumed pursuit with three more strokes, followed by one more for the defence, and so on until the bid was either hit or missed.

But whether these games of the Renaissance era bore any resemblance to golf is of little consequence, because by that time golf itself was well entrenched along the eastern coast of Scotland.

Indeed, the best argument for a true forefather of the Scottish game comes from the people across the North Sea, the Dutch, who back in the 13th century were playing a game that bears a more than passing similarity to golf. And the name of that game? Colf: spelt c–o–l–f.

As early as 1296 the Dutch had a colf course, and a formidable one at that. It stretched 4,500 yards for just four holes – except that they weren't holes, they were doors – to a kitchen, a windmill, a castle, and a courthouse. Four-door models such as this were

• Above
In the 18th century the Basques played a cross-country version of jeu de mail.

undoubtedly typical, but no target was off limits to the colf-crazed Dutchmen who pursued their balls through churchyards, cemeteries, and smack through the centres of their own towns, often wreaking havoc with the local citizenry. The winners usually collected a barrel of beer from the losing side, which means the original '19th Hole' actually was the fifth.

Ultimately, when the toll of personal injuries and broken glass became insupportable, the 'colfers' were banished to the countryside during the warmer months, and, in winter, to the frozen lakes and rivers where they directed their shots toward poles in the ice.

Numerous richly detailed landscape paintings drawn by the Dutch Masters show us that colf remained popular in Holland for at least 400 years. By the early 1700s, however, the game had mysteriously vanished.

Where did it go? In all probability, to Scotland. After all, it doesn't take a PhD in linguistics to make a connection between the words 'colf' and 'golf'. The implements used were very similar, the balls nearly identical. And above all, there is the compelling evidence of geography.

By 1650, golf – spelt as we know it today – was well-rooted in the fabric of a dozen or so cities along Scotland's east coast. One look at the map shows that the coast was a short sail from more than 40 commercial centres of Holland. Trade between the two countries was brisk, dating back to medieval times, and evidence exists that the Scots exported wooden golf clubs to the Dutch (along with wool and other products), while the Dutch returned with rudimentary colf balls.

And there are numerous paintings of the period showing Scotsmen in kilts playing a stick-and-ball game on the ice as the Dutch did.

But, no matter where the seeds of golf were sown, without question it was the Scots who gave the game its unique character, the Scots who combined the elements of distance off the tee and deftness around the green, and the Scots who ingrained the notion of each player advancing independently toward the hole, without interference from his opponents. (The Scots were largely Calvinists, who knew that the greatest sins, deserving

• Above
Colf was a recurrent subject in the landscapes of The Dutch Masters.

• Above
The marriage of Scotland's James IV to an English princess was good news for golfers.

• Below
Players at Blackheath, the first golf club in England.

the greatest punishment, always came from within. How perfectly this applies to golf.)

From the very beginning, this game was dangerously addictive. Indeed, the first written evidence of golf is a parliamentary decree banning it, for reasons of national security. In 1457 King James II of Scotland declared "that futeball and golfe be utterly cryit doune and nocht usit". Back then, the Scots were at war with England and the principal weapons of combat were the bow and arrow. But it seems the Scottish lads had been neglecting their archery practice in favour of golf.

Similar edicts were issued in the subsequent reigns of James III and IV...and were largely ignored. But when James IV married the daughter of England's King Henry IV, the conflict with the English suddenly ended – and so did the conflict with golfers. In fact, James IV himself became the first of a long line of royals who took to the links. In the account books of his court it is noted that funds were spent for the purchase of golf balls and clubs, and there also is the settling of a golf bet which the king lost. Legend also has it that in 1567 Mary Queen of Scots was so smitten with the game that she teed up the day after her husband, Lord Darnley, was murdered; this was, in fact, one of the charges levelled against her that eventually cost her the crown, her head, and a chance to win the return match.

In 1604, the King of England appointed a royal clubmaker, and soon after that, a seven-hole course was laid out near London on the Black Heath by the River Thames. Nearly 400 years later, Royal Blackheath still sits there, although it wasn't established as a club until 1766.

Despite the royal seal of approval, golf in those days was an equal opportunity pastime, open to anyone with a couple of clubs, a ball and the urge for some light exercise. One of the first written accounts of the game – a description of play on the Links of Leith, near Edinburgh – extols its democratic spirit:

"The greatest and wisest of the land were to be seen mingling freely with the humblest mechanics in the pursuit of their common and beloved amusement. All distinctions of rank were levelled by the joyous spirit of the game."

It was an informal, almost free-form activity back then, with no rules, few guidelines (although playing on the Sabbath was, for a time, illegal), and no tournaments or competitions except for casual matches among friends. All evidence suggests that the Scots played this disorganised brand of golf for at least three centuries.

Just as disorganised, certainly by modern standards, were the methods used to play the early game. Instead of one way to swing there were as many swings as there were villages with courses of their own. The townspeople tended to copy the technique of the local champion, who usually hit on a set-up and swing that allowed him to conquer the vagaries of the local weather.

The Scottish coast is constantly buffeted by sea breezes, so the most successful golfers learned to hit the ball on a low trajectory that kept it under the wind. To accomplish this, they learned to spread their feet far apart (as much as a yard), aim their bodies to the right of the target, position the ball well back in the stance, and bend their knees deeply. Then they whipped the club around their bodies (rather than up and down as we do today) on a markedly horizontal plane that further encouraged low flight. The ball flew just a few feet off the ground, travelling only about 150 yards, and would then run a long way after hitting the hard turf of the wind-blown links.

As the game spread, more methods and champions developed. Word of great play travelled from town to town. And, inevitably, a desire arose to determine the best golfer in the land. It was at that point that the game as we know it began to take shape.

In March of 1744, a group of golfers who played over the Links at Leith persuaded the city of Edinburgh to provide a silver club as the prize for an annual competition. The event was open to "as many Noblemen or Gentlemen or other Golfers, from any part of Great Britain or Ireland" as would send in their entries. The winner was to be called 'The Captain of the Golf', and would become the arbiter of all disputes touching the game.

The response was a bit underwhelming. Only a dozen men signed up – all of them local lads – and only ten played, with the prize going to an Edinburgh surgeon named John Rattray with a score of 60 for two trips around the five-hole course. That wasn't too bad considering the holes ranged from 414 to 495 yards, which one golf historian estimates would equal holes of 600 yards today, given our modern equipment. Nonetheless, this modest event is generally recognised as golf's first organised competition, and the Leith golfers are credited with forming the game's first bona fide club, the Honourable Company of Edinburgh Golfers. Over the next few generations, this group would move numerous times, always keeping their name intact, eventually settling to the east of Edinburgh at Muirfield, their current home, in 1891.

Ah, but on that day in 1744 something even

• Above
Parading the Silver Club, provided by the city of Edinburgh.

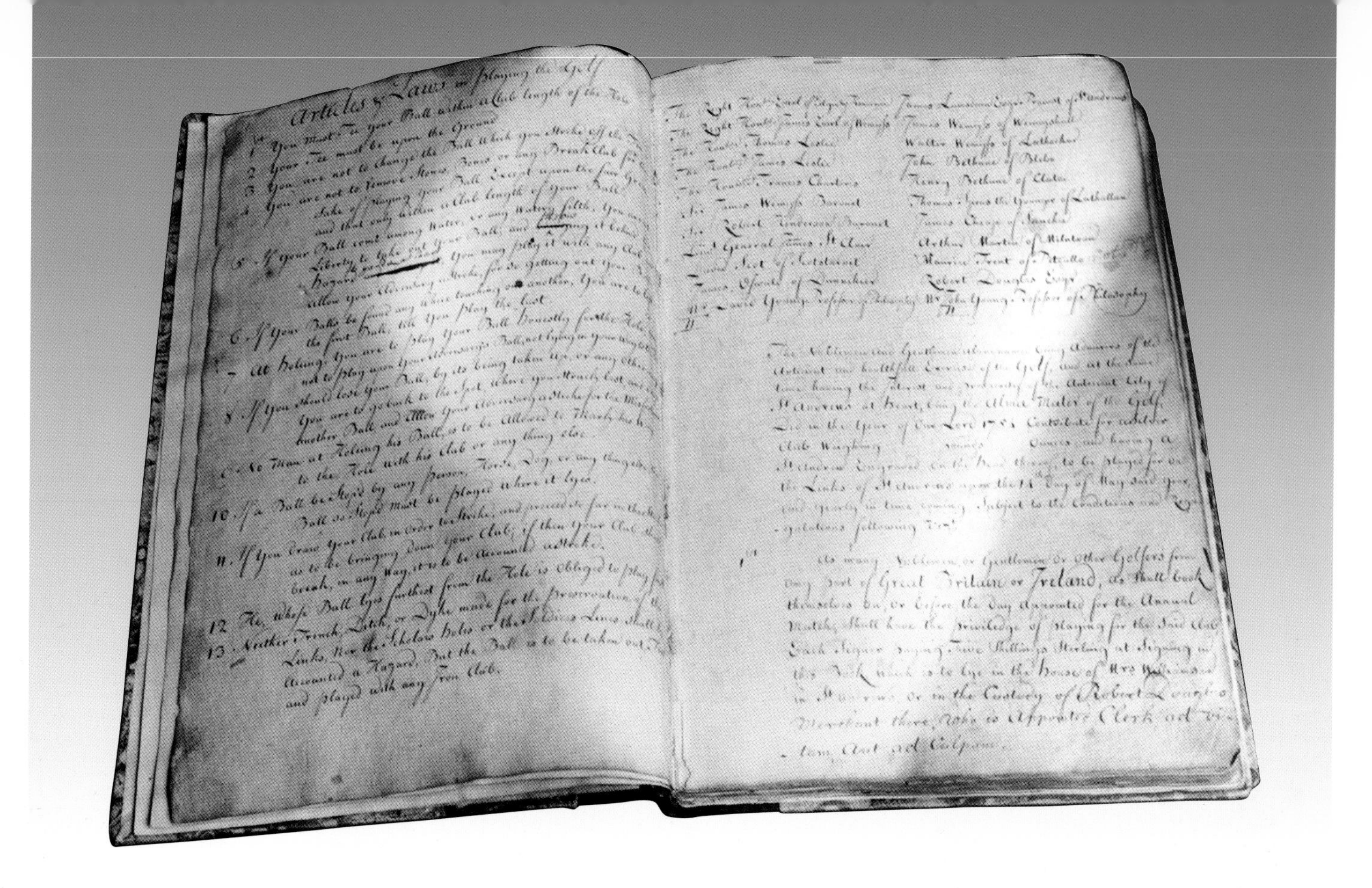

Articles & Laws in Playing the Golf

1. You Must Tee your Ball within a Club length of the Hole
2. Your Tee must be upon the Ground
3. You are not to change the Ball which you Strike off the Tee
4. You are not to Remove Stones, Bones or any Break Club for the sake of playing your Ball Except upon the fair Green and that only within a Club length of your Ball.
5. If your Ball come among Water, or any Watery filth, You are at liberty to take out your Ball, and bringing it behind the Hazard [illegible] You may play it with any Club and allow your Adversary a Stroke, for so getting out your Ball.
6. If your Balls be found any where touching one another, You are to lift the first Ball, till You play the last.
7. At Holing, You are to play your Ball Honestly for the Hole, and not to play upon your Adversary's Ball, not lying in your way to the Hole.
8. If you should lose your Ball, by its being taken up, or any other way, You are to go back to the Spot, where you Struck last, and drop another Ball and allow your Adversary a Stroke for the Misfortune.
9. No Man at Holing his Ball, is to be Allowed to Mark his way to the Hole with his Club or any thing else.
10. If a Ball be Stop'd by any person, Horse, Dog, or any thing else, The Ball so Stop'd must be played where it lyes.
11. If you draw your Club, in Order to Strike, and proceed so far in the Stroke as to be bringing down your Club; if then your Club shall break, in any way, it is to be Accounted a Stroke.
12. He, whose Ball lyes furthest from the Hole is Obliged to play first.
13. Neither Trench, Ditch, or Dyke made for the preservation of the Links, Nor the Scholars Holes or the Soldiers Lines, Shall be Accounted a Hazard, But the Ball is to be taken out, Teed and played with any Iron Club.

more important happened: golf was played for the first time according to a set of rules.

They were admirably brief – just 13 edicts in all (today's rule book is 120 pages long!) – and, admirably, charitable as well, with no penalties for violations. This set of simple, straightforward principles would prevail virtually unchanged for nearly a century.

Among the provisos: "If your ball is stopped by any person, horse, dog, or anything else, the ball must be played as it lies."; "if your club snaps and breaks in the course of the downswing, you are deemed to have made a stroke." And perhaps the most illuminating, the first rule: "You must tee your ball within a club-length of the hole." Imagine how frustratingly craggy those early putting greens must have been!

Indeed, golf's first playing fields bore little resemblance to the manicured meadows we enjoy today. The handful of courses that dotted the coast of Scotland were set on linksland, the barren, undulating, windswept terrain that separated the beach from the arable ground beyond. During the Ice Age, the sea had covered these areas, so the subsoil was sandy, which meant that it drained well but supported only long grasses and thick brush, making it of little value except as a home to rabbits and sheep.

In fact, it was these hungry herbivores who served as golf's first and most stalwart greenkeepers. Bear in mind that the game was played for about 400 years before any human got around to cutting the grass.

The animals also took a leading role in golf course design, by burrowing their way into the turf as protection against the elements. When, over time, the wind enlarged those burrows, golf's oldest and meanest hazard – the bunker – took shape.

Yes, those original courses were less fashioned by man than formed by nature. There were no tees, no fairways and no greens as such, just a hole in the ground every few hundred yards. And even those holes were a bit unpredictable. One might be as shallow as a rabbit scrape, the next so deep that simply retrieving one's ball was a major achievement.

There was no set number of holes for a round of golf, either. From town to town, variety was the name of the game as each course ran according to the flow of the land. A round thus consisted of one or more turns around whatever number of holes the locals happened to favour. While the Links at Leith was five holes, nearby North Berwick sported seven.

• Above
The Original 13 Rules of Golf, published in 1744.

Meanwhile, there was a 12-holer at Prestwick, on Scotland's west coast, and Montrose, on the North Sea, weighed in with a whopping 25.

In time, of course, a standard would be set. And the authority for that decree, as well as countless later rulings on the game, would come from the abiding bastion of golf administration, the town of St Andrews.

Set on a remote bulge of Scotland's east coast, this unassuming little town would seem a most unlikely seat of authority of any kind. Yet St Andrews had been the ecclesiastical heart of Scotland since the 12th century, a religious Mecca of equal stature to Canterbury in England. It is also the home of the oldest university in Scotland.

And, for generations of golfers, St Andrews has meant one thing: the grandest of all links, the Old Course, a magnificent stretch of rolling terrain set hard by a bay of the North Sea. Written evidence of golf at St Andrews dates from 1552, but most historians agree that the game was played there in one form or another for at least 300 years before that, perhaps by shepherds swinging crooks as the first clubs.

In 1890, Horace Hutchinson, an English essayist and inveterate St Andrews golfer, captured the cachet of the "Old Grey Toun" with words that ring equally true today: "When two stranger golfers meet upon some neutral ground, one of the first questions that will pass from one to the other will most certainly be 'Have you been to St Andrews?' and should the answer be in the negative the questioner will immediately deem himself justified in assuming a tone of patronage which the other will feel he has no right to resent."

The golfers of St Andrews did not organise themselves into a club until 1754, 10 years after the men of Leith. On May 14, "twenty-two Noblemen and Gentlemen being admirers of the ancient and healthful exercise of the Golf" formed The Society of St Andrews Golfers. They immediately adopted the

• ***Above***
Modern bunkers, a well-visited hazard on today's courses.

• ***Inset left***
Sheep – golf's first green-keepers.

• ***Inset right***
English essayist Horace Hutchinson was a dedicated St Andrews golfer.

The first step in that direction came in 1764 when the St Andreans made a drastic revision to their hallowed playground. At that time, the Old Course consisted of 12 holes, set in a long narrow strip along the shore. The golfers played 11 holes out to the far end of the course, then turned and threaded their way home, playing 10 of the holes backwards to the same cups before finishing at a solitary hole near where they'd started. Thus, a round at St Andrews consisted of 22 holes.

But in 1764, the Society of St Andrews Golfers decided to convert the first four holes of the course into two. This trimming may have been precipitated by a record round: earlier that year, William St Clair played the 22 holes in 121 strokes, an average of 5.5 strokes per hole. Since this change automatically shortened the same four holes to two on the road in, the St Andrews round was reduced from 22 holes to 18, the number that would become standard throughout the world. (Due to subsequent changes, including widening the fairways and enlarging the greens, the Old Course that we know today wasn't really in play until the early 1840s.) Over the following years, the Society would attract

13 rules set down by the golfers of Edinburgh. They also adopted the Honourable Company's habit of dressing for play in bright red coats, the better to be seen by the locals, who used the same linksland for strolling, doing the laundry, and picnicking. But despite following Edinburgh's lead, it was almost inevitable that this small town would assume an administrative role equal to the stature it had already earned, as the golf capital of the world.

• ***Above***
A 1798 competition among members of the Society of St Andrews Golfers.

• ***Below***
The impressive and unmistakable clubhouse at St Andrews.

the best and brightest golfers and gentlemen, frame a new set of rules, and generally position itself as the last word on all questions related to the game, even setting the standard for the size of the cups cut in the green (4 ¼in). When, in 1834, England's King William IV became the patron of the Society and declared it the Royal & Ancient Golf Club, the enduring pre-eminence of St Andrews was assured.

Back in 1834, however, there wasn't much golf to oversee. Only 17 clubs existed: 14 of them in Scotland, two in England, and one in India, at the Royal Calcutta Golf Club, where a group of British colonials had brought the game.

In all the world at that time, fewer than a thousand people could call themselves golfers. And more than a few were women.

In 1811, the fishwives of Musselburgh participated in the first known women's tournament. The first club for women, the St Andrews Ladies' Golf Club, was formed in 1867 and boasted a membership of over 500 by 1886. The Ladies' Golf Union followed in 1893, with the first official Ladies Championship not far behind. It was won, as were the two that followed, by the remarkable Lady Margaret Scott, who was known for an unusually long backswing (the club nearly hit her in the back), tremendous distance (gained, perhaps, from trying to keep up with three golfer brothers), and scores in the 80s, all while wearing the long skirts, long sleeves, and other less-than-sporting attire expected of a woman in that era. Not much more is known about her other than that after winning her third straight championship, Lady Margaret married and retired from the game undefeated.

Doing somewhat less well, however, was the game itself. In the early 1800s golf wasn't spreading, it was shrinking. What a century earlier had been a recreation of the masses had eroded into a diversion for the wealthy and privileged.

Why?

Above all, because of the ball.

• Above
The Westward Ho Ladies Golf Club at Bideford, Devon in 1873.

• Below
King William IV declared St Andrews the Royal and Ancient Golf Club.

Development of the Game

Chapter TWO

2

TELEGRAMS: PARK, LINKS, MUSSELBURGH

MEMO. from

Wm Park & Son of Scotland

Golf Club & Ball Manufacturers.

BRANCHES: MUSSELBURGH LINKS, NORTH BERWICK, 6, SOUTH ST ANDREW ST, EDINBURGH. and NEW YORK.

CHAMPION GOLFERS 1860·1863·1866·1875·1887·1889·

Speciality: Park's Patent Putter.

Links, MUSSELBURGH, 190

M

The very first golfers are believed to have played with balls made of boxwood, similar to the balls used in the earlier games of pall mall and chole. The balls were simply turned on a carpenter's lathe, and, if a bit lacking in sophistication, were at least affordable.

But in the early 17th century a new ball was put in play. Called the feathery, it consisted of a leather cover stuffed with the breast feathers of a goose or chicken. It was about 1.6in in diameter (roughly the size that the ball is today), but weighed only three-quarters of an ounce, about half that of a modern ball. The feathery provided good resilience and distance: the strongest players could hit it over 200 yards. But with this development, the making of golf balls suddenly became a fine art.

A strip of untanned bull or horse hide was soaked in alum water, then cut into three pieces – two circles and a strip for the middle. These were sewn together, soaked again, and turned inside out so the seams were on the inside. A small hole was left in this shell, and into that hole the ballmaker stuffed the feathers, which had been boiled to make them limp and malleable. He did his stuffing with the aid of a tool called a 'brogue', a blunt-edged iron spike topped with a wooden crosspiece on which the ballmaker leaned with all his weight. When he had crammed in approximately a top hat-full of feathers using the brogue, he poked in a last few with a small awl and then sewed up the hole.

Then, still wet inside and out, the ball was set out to dry. As it did, the feathers expanded while the cover contracted, thus producing a sphere of resilient hardness. The feathery was then hammered as round as possible, and painted for protection against the elements.

Feathery making was a serious business requiring equal parts mastery and muscle, and even the best craftsmen could produce no more than four balls per day. Accordingly, featheries were extremely expensive – 12 times more costly than the old wooden balls.

What's more, for all that work, the finished product was less than a model of durability. It became waterlogged easily and one off-centre slash with an iron club could literally knock the stuffing out of it. Thus, a player invariably required three or four

• Top
One of the most famous early suppliers of golf products was Willie Park & Son.

• Above
Expensive to manufacture, featheries, early golf balls, around 1850.

• Below right
Gutta Percha balls from around 1890, later known as 'gutties', restored the game to the masses.

balls per round.

Under these circumstances, only the wealthiest golfers could sustain their passion. Clearly, what was needed was a ball that would be inexpensive, weatherproof and more rounded; a ball whose performance, durability and affordability would attract more people to the game.

In the mid-19th century, that ball arrived. It came all the way from the Far East in the form of gutta percha, the coagulated milk of a Malayan gum tree.

The precise origin of the gutta percha ball is a matter of some dispute, but surely the claim that is most exotic, if not authentic, is the saga of the Hindu statue. It seems that James Paterson, a Scottish missionary based in India, sent a statue – actually a marble bas relief of the Hindu god Vishnu – to his brother Robert, then a ministry student in St Andrews. The statue had been cushioned for shipment with chunks and chips of gutta percha, a pliable substance that so fascinated young Robert that he first tried to resole his boot with it. Then he fashioned it into a golf ball.

Robert Paterson played a few holes on the Old Course with his gutta percha ball in April 1845, without great consequence, then sent the ball to a third brother near Edinburgh who took up the cause and began producing gutta percha balls as a business venture.

The substance was exported in the form of a sheet which the ballmaker cut into strips, softened in hot water, and rounded into a ball by hand. The ball was then dropped into cold water to harden. It was as simple as that. And if a 'gutty' became a little bruised or cracked, it could be re-softened in hot water and made whole again.

The first gutties brought mixed reaction. They were certainly rounder than the feather ball – in fact they were nearly as smooth as billiard balls – but therein lay a problem. With no markings on their surface, they were tough to get airborne and tended to duck or dive in flight. Yet golfers didn't know that – yet.

Willie Dunn, a professional at Musselburgh, was so disgusted with the gutties' poor flight that he gave the balls to his caddies. In short time, however, he noticed the caddies were hitting the gutty with more authority than he himself could muster from a feathery. The reason proved to be the nicks and scuffs the ball had received from iron shots: once it had a few cuts on its face, the gutty flew like a champion. Thus, generation two became the hand-hammered gutty, with aerodynamic markings pre-chiseled on its surface.

Here, then, was a ball that travelled farther, putted truer and, best of all, cost far less than its feather-stuffed forerunner. In short time, entire Malayan forests were being levelled for the sake of golf, as craftsmen began cranking out gutties at the rate of a hundred a day. Armed with this ball for all, thousands of tradesmen, artisans and peasants once again joined their better-bred brethren on the links as golf returned at last to the working man.

By 1890, the smattering of golf clubs in Great Britain would grow to 387, playing over 140 different courses. Meanwhile, outside the UK golf would extend its colonial tentacles to every outpost in the British Empire, reaching Australia, New Zealand, Canada, South Africa, Ceylon, Shanghai, Bangkok and Hong Kong, as well as India. A gutta percha golf boom had reignited the game.

But the arrival of the gutty was met with alarm and opposition by one faction of the golf world: the feathery makers. Chief among them was the game's first renaissance man, Allan Robertson of St Andrews.

A sturdily-built fellow with red-brown whiskers and a perpetual smile, Allan was the last of six generations of club- and ballmaking Robertsons, and was also the finest golfer of his time, purportedly never losing a head-to-head match. In Reminiscences of Golf on St Andrews Links, published in 1887, James Balfour described Robertson thus: "He was a short, little, active man, with a pleasant face, small features and a merry twinkle in his eye. He was universally popular, not a bit forward, but withal easy and full of self-respect." Robertson is credited with

• Above
Allan Robertson was the game's first great player. Tradition has it that he was never beaten as an individual when playing for money.

being the game's first professional player (meaning he played for money) and was probably the game's first course architect and green superintendent as well, rendering an unofficial but highly valued service as tender of the St Andrews links.

But ballmaking was Robertson's livelihood, and the gutty threatened it. At one point he became so bitter that he bought up any gutties found in the bushes of the Old Course and destroyed them by fire. Robertson also made his employees promise never to use the ball, which led to a rift between him and his chief apprentice, Tom Morris.

Six years Robertson's junior and nearly as fine a player, Morris agreed to shun the gutty, but then was caught in a transgression. He pleaded innocence, claiming he'd run out of featheries in mid-round and was forced to borrow a ball, but Robertson was unconvinced. The result was that Morris left his employer and opened his own shop, making gutties, first in St Andrews and later in Prestwick, where he also became keeper of the green.

In time, however, even Robertson gave in to the gutty, happily finding that he could produce more balls – and income – with much less work. And, to his credit, he was among the first to realise that the new ball required a new set of clubs.

Golf had been played with essentially the same implements for more than two centuries, an assortment of idiosyncratic mallets devised to fit the rugged demands of the game. The woods, which far outnumbered the irons, had shafts made of hazelwood or ash with heads of apple or thornwood, materials hard enough to withstand impact first with wooden balls, then the alum-hardened featheries. The two pieces of wood were carefully spliced together, then glued and bound with several windings of tarred twine. The grips were soft sheepskin wrapped around the end of the shaft.

The biggest wallop was packed by the play club, a long-nosed weapon with little or no loft in its tiny, 1in high hitting area. Its shaft was 45in long, about the same as today's drivers, but it met the clubhead at an angle of 120 degrees, forcing the early golfers to stand well away from the ball and contributing to the flat,

around-the-body sweeping swing. The sole of the clubface was reinforced with the most exotic of materials, a strip of ram's horn.

A variety of lofted woods – called spoons, because their faces were curved like the bowl of a spoon to create loft – were used for approach play, from the long spoon for distance shots to the baffing spoon for raising the ball from poor lies and over hazards. Putters were also made of wood, and a single golfer might carry as many as three of them: in addition to the traditional putter for holing out there was the driving putter for hitting low tee shots into the wind and the approach putter for bumping the ball in to the green. All of the putters were lofted, at least in part to limit the time the ball was in contact with the unmanicured fairways and greens of the day.

Iron clubs, being hazardous to the health of the feather ball, were few and reserved for only the direst of circumstances, as suggested by their names: bunker iron, rut iron and track iron. Their heads were bizarre-looking things with concave faces and snubbed-off toes that suited the nasty assignments for which they were intended. Since Allan Robertson and his contemporaries had little expertise in metalworking, the heads were forged in blacksmith's shops and then supplied to the clubmakers, who riveted them to the wooden shafts.

But, as the ball changed, so did the clubs. The gutty was much harder than the feathery and it yielded very little at impact. When the traditional wood clubs made forceful contact with the gutty they tended to split and crack. Something had to give, and it was, of course, the clubs, which began to appear with shafts of a softer wood – hickory – imported from American forests. The new shafts also had less torsion: the clubhead lagged less far behind the hands during the downswing, which would eventually lead to a change in swing technique to a more up-and-down attack on the ball.

The clubheads changed also, to a softer beechwood to better absorb the hit, and became shorter and thicker to pack more punch directly behind the ball. Strips of leather were inset in the clubface, which otherwise became worn and dented from constant collision with the gutty. The ultimate effect of all of this was to lessen the strain on the weakest part of the club, the spliced area just above the clubhead.

Meanwhile, iron clubs came into their own. No longer a menace to the ball, they became the preferred implements for approach shots of every kind. Indeed, such was the growth in demand for irons that several Scottish blacksmiths abandoned their other areas of trade and took up clubmaking full-time, under the title 'cleekmaker'. The cleek – equivalent to the modern 2 or 3-iron – was the first

• Opposite
'Old' Tom Morris was sacked from his job as a feathery maker after being caught playing a gutty ball.

• Above
The assembly line at an early cleekmaker's shop.

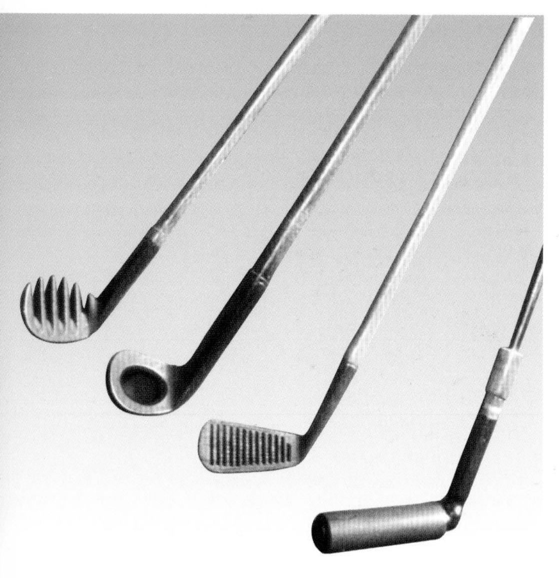

• Above
Tom Auchterlonie of St Andrews, among the best known craftsmen.

• Below
Bizarre early irons, weapons against the tougher shots!

to appear and was followed swiftly by the progressively more lofted mid-iron, mashie, and niblick. All of which eventually led to perhaps the most practical invention of all – a simple sailcloth golf bag.

One of the first bags is said to have been constructed by Bryant Andrews, the keeper of the clubhouse at Westward Ho!, the old links course along the southwest coast of England. Andrews, a former sailor and sailmaker, sewed some pieces of sailcloth together, figuring that the "circular shape would have the effect of enclosing the greater part of the clubshafts and thus preventing the grips from getting wet". The golf bag made its commercial debut in England in 1891; called a 'carrier', it usually came fitted with a stake or arrangement of legs so it could stand or lean on its own.

Allan Robertson embraced the new irons both as a craftsman and a player, and was probably the first to master the run-up shot with a cleek. It was at St Andrews, in September 1858, he ran his approach onto the 18th green, then rolled in his gutty for a birdie and a total of 79, making him the first man to break 80 on the Old Course.

A year later, Robertson fell sick with hepatitis and died at the age of 44. Among the tributes to him: "They may toll the bells and shut up their shops in St Andrews, for their greatest is gone."

Robertson's death left a void at the top of professional golf, and there was soon an urge to fill it. By now, the game had spread sufficiently through Scotland to produce a group of highly skilled players, with Tom Morris and Musselburgh's Willie Park leading the pack. At the same time, expanded rail travel had brought the top players and courses within easy train reach of each other.

So, in 1860, the Prestwick Club, on the west coast, took the first step by announcing a championship for professional golfers. To the winner they offered a unique prize: a red Moroccan leather

belt, embroidered with silver medallions.

Permanent possession of the belt would go to whomever was capable of winning the title three years in succession.

Only eight men entered that first event, and the lowest score among them came from Willie Park with 174 for 36 holes, a rather high total even for those days. Tom Morris was next at 176 over the 12-hole, 3,803-yard circuit. In fact, the scores were so high that a number of amateurs felt they might do better, and so the next year the competition was opened to all. And it has remained just so – the Open Championship, or, as Americans know it, the British Open.

Tom Morris won the title the following year and he and Willie Park would split seven of the first eight, with Morris taking four and Park three. (The tournament was played at Prestwick from 1860 to 1872.) When Morris won for the last time, in 1868 at the age of 46, he became, and still remains, the oldest Open Champion.

One year later, the title was won by a lad of 17

• ***Above***
The famous 'Alps' hole from Prestwick, home of the first 12 Opens.

• ***Below***
Old Willie Park who, with Old Tom Morris, would split seven of the first eight Opens.

years who became, and still remains, the youngest Open Champion. His name also was Tom Morris. This legendary father-son duo would forever be known as Old and Young Tom.

Young Tom Morris was as wonderfully gifted a player as the game had ever seen or ever would. A broad-shouldered lad, he could hit the ball with tremendous power, making him a master of the recovery from trouble, but he was also a skilful pitcher and putter, and is credited with inventing the lofted pitch shot. In truth, his game had no weakness, as he proved by defending his title successfully in 1869 and then taking permanent possession of the belt with a third straight win in 1870. On the first hole of that 1870 Open – a monster of 570 yards – Young Tom posted a 3, a score that would be equivalent to an albatross today. He won the title by 12 strokes with a then astounding total of 149, a mark that would stand for 34 years. He also won numerous head-to-head matches, many for big purses, against the other great players of the day. He single-handedly beat the better ball of teams of the best players, and often teaming up with his father, played challenge matches that they nearly always won.

There was a gap in Open play in 1871 because no one came forward to offer a prize to replace the belt. Then, in 1872, a silver claret jug was presented jointly by St Andrews, Musselburgh and Prestwick, and the three sites began a club-to-club rotation that continues today, although there are now more clubs and a less strict order of rotation.

When the Open competition resumed, 'Tommy' picked up where he'd left off, winning the title at Prestwick for a fourth time. He might well have won it at least another four more times, too, had he not died suddenly at the age of 24.

It is still one of the saddest tales in the game's long history. In September of 1875 Old and Young Tom were playing the brothers Willie and Mungo Park in a big-money match at North Berwick, across the Firth of Forth from St Andrews. Just as the Morrises were closing out the match on the 18th green, Old Tom received a telegram; he wouldn't tell his son why, but they had to leave immediately on a

• Inset
First prize in the Open was a red leather belt embossed with silver medallions.

• Above
The belt retired with Young Tom when in 1870 he won the title for a third straight time.

• Opposite
'Young' Tom died of a broken heart aged 24 after his wife and newborn died in childbirth.

yacht put at their disposal by a wealthy friend. As they cut across the waves, Young Tom learned from his father that his wife and newborn had died in childbirth. It was a blow from which the young man never recovered. He played golf only twice more and then, on Christmas Eve, he passed away mysteriously in his sleep. The clinical cause of his death was likely pneumonia, but, in the lore of golf, Young Tom Morris died of a broken heart. One of the largest monuments in the cemetery in St Andrews is for Young Tom. It reads, in part: "In Memory of Tommy, son of Thomas Morris…Deeply regretted by numerous friends and all golfers. He thrice in succession won the champion's belt and held it without rivalry and yet without envy. His many amiable qualities being no less acknowledged than his golfing achievements…."

Old Tom would outlive his son by 33 years, and for the last half of his life he returned to his native St Andrews as the first resident professional to the Royal & Ancient Golf Club. With his long grey beard, tweed cap and pipe, Tom Morris was a familiar figure to all who passed by his shop near the 18th green.

Spreading the Gospel of Golf

Chapter THREE

3

A royal interest in golf was undoubtedly one of the prime factors in spreading the popularity of this ancient game, but golf took its time reaching the masses. When it did, however, the game spread like wildfire. The period in time from the middle of the 19th century to the beginning of the next witnessed an explosion in golf's popularity and, crucially, its participation.

The statistics behind golf's growth are remarkable. Around the year 1860 there were only 30 golf clubs in Scotland and just three in England. By 1900 there were more than 2,000 golf clubs spread far and wide across the whole of Britain. There were not quite as many actual courses, for at that time it was common practice for golf clubs to share the same course. Nevertheless, the trend was undeniably strong. A new club had been established every single week of the year for nearly half-a-century; golf had truly gripped the nation.

There were two main driving forces behind the golf boom. First, and perhaps most significantly of all, the recently introduced gutty ball was much cheaper than the feathery which it replaced – in fact, about a quarter of the price – which brought the game within the financial reach of a far wider audience. Suddenly, the ordinary working man could play the game. Also, the gutty was easier to manufacture and therefore could be made in sufficient quantities to meet the increased demand for golf balls.

The expansion of the railways was the second major influence. With travel being that much easier, and again within the means of a far wider audience, more and more people started to take holidays. The seaside resorts built golf courses as a way to attract visitors. It proved to be a fruitful period.

This golden age saw the birth of some classic layouts which share not only a royal patronage, but their proximity to the sea – on linksland, rugged and natural terrain that Mother Nature must surely have set aside purely for the purposes of playing golf. The list of courses built in the latter part of the 19th century is as long as it is inspiring: Royal North Devon (1864), Royal Liverpool (1869), Royal Dornoch (1877), Royal Troon (1878), Royal Lytham & St Annes (1886), Royal St George's (1887), Royal Birkdale (1889), Royal Cinque Ports (1892), and Royal West Norfolk (1892). More than a century after their creation, these golf courses have a timeless appeal which draws visitors from all over the world. The

• Above
A general view of the Royal Troon golf course and clubhouse.

game may well be royal and ancient, but the means by which golfers indulge their passion is very 21st century.

While the golf-course boom continued apace, so the Open Championship in its new incarnation went from strength to strength. From 1872, a steadily increasing number of entrants competed for the Claret Jug, a trophy which would soon become the most famous in the world of golf. With Old Tom Morris past his competitive best, and his son tragically dying while at the peak of his powers, it was left to a new guard to take over.

Jamie Anderson, a St Andrews man, was the first to seize the opportunity. He won the championship three times in a row from 1877–79, the last of those being on his home golf course. Bob Ferguson followed, himself completing an impressive hat-trick of Open victories from 1880–82. When the championship came to his home course, Musselburgh, in 1883 Ferguson could so easily have made it four in a row, but much to his disappointment, and no doubt the locals, he came to grief in a playoff against Willie Fernie.

The performances of two great amateurs lit up the Open Championship in the final decade of the 19th century. John Ball, who in 1890 became the first golfer from outside Scotland to take the Claret Jug, was an incredibly successful amateur. He won the Amateur Championship an amazing eight times in a period spanning a quarter of a century.

He was a formidable opponent and one of the finest shot makers of his day, adept at getting himself out of all manner of trouble and inventing shots to suit the conditions. Ball could make the golf ball talk, even if he himself wasn't overly keen to do so. Indeed, he was a shy, modest character. His nature would have no doubt suited an anonymous life, but his superb golf game guaranteed that could never be the case.

In Ball's footsteps followed Harold Hilton, another Englishman and the second amateur to win the Open Championship. Like Ball, he learnt his craft at the Royal Liverpool Golf Club, but their games were quite dissimilar. Hilton had a decidedly inelegant golf swing. Bernard Darwin described it thus: "A little man jumping on his toes and throwing himself and his club after the ball with almost frantic abandon." But no one could say it wasn't effective.

His first Open victory at Muirfield in 1892, the

• ***Above***
John Ball became the first golfer from outside Scotland to take the Claret Jug.

• ***Inset***
Jamie Anderson won three consecutive Open Championships from 1877.

first year the championship was extended to 72 holes, was sealed with a total of 305 which wasn't bettered for more than a decade. Hilton went on to win the championship for a second time, at his home club Royal Liverpool, in 1897.

Hilton also won the Amateur Championship four times and was runner-up three times. Arguably his most impressive achievement, however, did not take place on home soil, but on the other side of the Atlantic. It was in 1911 that he won the US Amateur Championship. He is the only Brit ever to do so.

Golf in Britain was soaring to new heights of popularity and awareness, yet in America it had barely even taken off. It fell upon the influence of Old Tom Morris to play an indirect, but crucial, role in changing that. For the last half of his life, having returned to his beloved St Andrews, Old Tom was the first resident professional at the Royal & Ancient Golf Club. With his distinctive long grey beard, tweed cap and pipe, he was a familiar figure to all who passed by his shop near the 18th green.

One of those visitors, during the late summer of 1887, was a gentleman named Robert Lockhart. A native of nearby Dunfermline, Lockhart had emigrated to the United States, but his job as a linen merchant frequently took him back to his home soil. Lockhart had learned to play golf as a boy on the links at Musselburgh, and in 1886 he decided to introduce the game to his friends in America. So, in Tom Morris' shop, he purchased six clubs and two dozen gutta percha balls. Six months later, on the morning of George Washington's birthday in 1888, Lockhart's friend and fellow Scotsman John Reid assembled with five other gentlemen in a cow pasture in New York, to give golf a try.

All six became instant converts, and although their progress was halted briefly by the notorious Blizzard of '88, they soon resumed play with frequency and fervour. In the autumn of that year they assembled at Reid's home and founded a club which, in honour of the home of golf, they named the St Andrew's Golf Club. It is that day – November 14, 1888 – that historians agree with virtual unanimity was the official beginning of golf in the United States.

And so it was that John Reid became the Father of American Golf, with his band of pilgrims becoming known as The Apple Tree Gang, thanks to the fruit-bearing specimen that served as their makeshift clubhouse. A wide wooden seat encircled the trunk, while in its branches the members hung their coats, their lunch containers, and a wicker basket holding several pints of Scotland's other great gift to the world.

• Above
Harold Hilton won the Open twice, the Amateur Championship four times and most impressively is still the only ever British winner of the US Amateur title.

At that time, in fact, apple trees were the defining element of the St Andrew's course, perched as it was on a 34-acre orchard overlooking the Hudson River. Indeed, so imposing were the trees that newcomers to golf in the US assumed them to be integral features of any reputable course. An early story involves one Judge O'Brien who, having niblicked his way through his first round of golf at St Andrew's, made a visit to the Shinnecock Hills Golf Club on the barren and windblown turf of Eastern Long Island. Upon seeing that layout for the first time, the judge declared with full confidence that it "was not a golf course at all because it had no apple trees over which to loft and play."

But other courses were sprouting in America – with and without apple trees – and they were sprouting quickly. Within five years of the founding of St Andrew's, dozens of clubs had opened, aided by a steady stream of emigrant Scottish professionals. A standing joke of the era was the availability of a club professional's job for anyone coming off the boat with the name Willie and a sufficiently thick Scottish brogue!

Willie Dunn went to Shinnecock, Willie Campbell to Brookline in Massachusetts, Willie Anderson to Apawamis in New York and Willie Smith to Midlothian in Illinois. The tiny Scottish town of Carnoustie alone would ship more than 250 men to golf professional jobs at early American clubs.

Scots had also emigrated to all corners of the British Empire, spreading the gospel of golf to an ever-expanding audience. Golf courses were popping up everywhere. India was the first to receive golf, with the opening of the Royal Calcutta Golf Club. It then quickly spread to Australia, with the forming of Royal Melbourne in 1891 and Royal Adelaide and Royal Sydney in the following two years. New Zealand was next on golf's great expansion plan, as were Mauritius, Canada, Hong Kong, and South Africa. In continental Europe, too, golf was getting a grip. France and Belgium were among the first to embrace the game and build golf courses.

Whilst many of the Open champions and leading Scottish professionals were in a hurry to get to the United States, one fellow, Charles Blair Macdonald, went the other way. The son of a wealthy Chicagoan,

• ***Pictures***
The "Father of American Golf", John Reid of Dunfermline.

• Above
Iron-willed Charles Blair Macdonald won the first US Amateur title in 1895.

Macdonald sailed to St Andrews in 1872 at the age of 16 to study at the university. The day after he arrived, Macdonald was taken to the shop of Old Tom Morris where his grandfather bought him a set of clubs. Within short time the youngster was spending every spare moment playing the Old Course and listening to and learning from the great players of the day, including both Old and Young Tom.

Two years later, Macdonald returned to the States with a passion for the game and strong convictions about every aspect of it. But, since the US was devoid of courses at the time, he made do for 15 years playing only on business trips to Britain. Once America got the golf bug, however, Macdonald was ready. When, in 1894 a group of the best amateurs assembled at the Newport Golf Club in Rhode Island to determine a national champion, CB was the man to beat.

But he did not win – with a score of 189 for 36 holes, he lost by a stroke to one of the Newport members, William Lawrence. Macdonald later protested that a stone wall, which had cost him two strokes in the second round, was not a legitimate hazard under the Rules of Golf. He also claimed that a proper championship should not be a matter of who takes the fewest strokes but should be decided in a head-to-head format.

The following month he got his wish when the St Andrew's Golf Club held a second amateur championship, this one at matchplay. Macdonald defeated his Newport nemesis Lawrence in the semi-finals, but, after halving the 18-hole final match, he sliced his drive into a ploughed field on the first hole of a playoff and lost to Lawrence Stoddard of the host club.

This time he argued that the result was invalid because one club may not presume to run a national championship. Macdonald's gripes were largely self-serving, but he was a man with a commanding presence – broad-shouldered, thickly moustached, well-spoken and humourless – and he got his points across to the right people.

Lawrence Curtis, the man who started golf at The Country Club in Brookline, Massachusetts, spoke to Henry Tallmadge, one of the founders of St Andrew's, and they agreed to invite representatives of various clubs to form a central body with authority to conduct national

championships and otherwise further the interests of the game. And so in December of 1894, over dinner at The Calumet Club in New York City, the United States Golf Association was founded.

Macdonald undoubtedly wanted to be the association's first president, but was far too contentious a character for the job. It went instead to a Newport business titan named Theodore Havemeyer, with CB settling for second vice-president.

A year later, however, Macdonald got what he really wanted – a victory in the USGA's first Amateur Championship. It was held at Newport in October, having been pushed back a month so as not to intrude on a more important event, the Americas Cup race.

Twenty-nine gentleman golfers took part and Macdonald, more determined than ever, blazed to a 12&11 victory in the final match over Charles Sands, a young tennis buff who had entered the championship as a lark, having played golf for all of three months.

On the next day, a much quieter event came to pass when a 21-year-old Englishman named Horace Rawlins bettered a field of nine fellow professionals and one amateur to become the first United States Open Champion. Although it is now one of the most coveted titles in golf, the US Open back then was little more than an afterthought.

CB Macdonald's breakthrough was also his swansong – he would contend in other championships but never win again. Macdonald, however, would have a continued and lasting influence on the game, as America's first great golf course architect. It was CB, in fact, who coined the term "golf architect".

In 1895 his bold design at the Chicago Golf Club – a seaside-type course set a thousand miles from the nearest sea – became the first 18-hole course in America. But Macdonald's undisputed masterpiece was a layout on the eastern end of Long Island, a course which – with typical pomposity – he named The National Golf Links of America.

Macdonald poured several years of his life and many thousands of his dollars into it, and in its rolling fairways and imaginatively contoured greens he brought to bear the full measure of his St Andrews training. When the National opened in 1911 it set a new standard for American golf architecture, and nearly a century later it continues to rank among the top 20 courses in the world. Inside the clubhouse is a life-sized bronze statue of CB Macdonald. Legend claims he commissioned it himself and then billed the membership for it.

Whether that is true or not, CB's ego was insatiable, and he wasn't afraid to feed it in the design of his courses. A notorious slicer, he routed the Chicago Golf Club's holes in a clockwise circle to favour the left-to-right drift of his shots. Spray the ball to the right and your worst penalty was light rough. Spray it left and you were flailing through a cornfield.

• Above
Englishman Horace Rawlins won the first US Open in 1895.

• Above
The Haskell ball transformed the game at the beginning of the 20th century.

Since this inequity was simply too severe, a three-word phrase made its debut in the rule book of 1899: out of bounds. Thereafter, those whose shots flew too far afield were allowed to re-tee the ball, at a penalty of one stroke.

Golf at the turn of the century was healthy – so healthy that, according to one physician it threatened the health of its devotees. In a 1901 report, Dr AC Bernays of St Louis attributed the death of one Wayman McCreery to an overindulgence in golf. It seems the obese Mr McCreery had shed a quick 38 pounds by playing a ferocious schedule of rounds, but had died shortly thereafter. Said the doctor, "The golf fad for busy men who have become corpulent is a dangerous experiment, and the sad example of Mr McCreery must be a warning for all."

Undaunted, Americans took to the links with Yankee tenacity. They didn't want simply to play, they wanted to play with the graceful pivot, dazzling footwork and overlapping grip that Harry Vardon had made famous. However, while the great man's technique was much admired, the famous golf ball that bore his name, the Vardon Flyer, had about flown its last. Another new ball made its way to the tee. And it would change everything.

Coburn Haskell was a bicycle maker, outdoors man, horse racer, and entrepreneur. He was also the shortest hitter in his foursome at the Portage Golf Club near Cleveland, Ohio, and, like every golfer before and after him, he daydreamed of longer drives. One day, while visiting the office of his friend Bertram Work, an engineer with the BF Goodrich rubber company, Haskell noticed a scrap basket full of elastic thread. Instantly he had a brainstorm – he could wind those thin strands of rubber around an inner core and make a golf ball, the same way a baseball was wound with wool thread. Such a ball would surely be more resilient and lively than a gutty.

Indeed, but wrapping several hundred feet of elastic into a neat little sphere was easier said than done. Years later, Bertram Work described his friend's early frustration: "He would get the thing wound about half way and then it would leap out of his hands and go bounding about the room, unwinding naturally with Haskell scrambling after it and cursing."

But Haskell stuck with his concept, eventually getting a ball wadded up, and convincing Work's company to fashion a gutta percha cover for it. The result was America's first major golf invention and perhaps the single most important contribution in the history of the game: the Haskell ball. It flew fully 20 yards farther than the gutty, and it hit the ground running. Initially, in fact, this increased bounce and roll made the Haskell difficult to control, especially around the green, and for a time many players carried an old-style gutty, just for chipping and putting.

But, for ladies, older players and anyone in dire need of distance, the Haskell made golf a whole different game. After short-hitting Walter Travis used it to win the 1901 US Amateur, the ball known as "Bounding Billy" was embraced by America and within short time the Goodrich Company was mass-producing them on an automatic winding machine.

The British were more skittish, with one critic dismissing the Haskell as "the ball for a tired man". Among the most vocal opponents was Sandy Herd, a perennial contender for the Open Championship who, on the eve of the 1902 championship, denounced the ball as unfit and expressed the hope that every other professional in the field would play it, as he most certainly would not.

But a funny thing happened on his way to the first tee. During a practice round, Herd got a quick lesson on playing the Haskell, from the appropriately named amateur ace John Ball, and suddenly Sandy changed his mind. The result was that the 1902 British Open went to Sandy Herd by one stroke over Harry Vardon, still flogging the ill-fated Flyer.

Incredibly, Herd had used the same ball for all 72 holes, and just as incredibly, he had been the only player in the field to play a Haskell. Shortly thereafter, Horace Hutchinson wrote on behalf of his countrymen, "We accept the American invention, as Britons will, of course, with grumbling, but with gratitude deep in our hearts." And so, from both sides of the Atlantic, the message was the same: Good-bye, gutty.

• Above
Sandy Herd made a last-minute switch to the Haskell ball and won the 1902 Open.

The Haskellisation of golf changed everything, beginning with the implements that struck the new ball. The softer, more springy Haskell required woods with a harder hit, and persimmon became the tree of choice, with inserts of various materials adding to the smack. Iron heads were enlarged and scored with grooves to help impart backspin, and clubs with extra loft were added as suddenly the key was not simply to make the ball go but also to make it stop.

The ball also turned out to be salvo number one in an endless game of attack-and-defend between golf technology and course design. Up to this time, American golf architecture had been a matter of quantity rather than quality, with the demand for places to play far surpassing the talent to design them well. As an adjunct to Vardon's tour, Spalding had dispatched a chap named Tom Bendelow across America to serve as architect for anyone who wanted a course. Bendelow had no particular knowledge or training – he was a typesetter for The New York Herald – but he had an authentic Scottish accent and he worked cheaply, just $25 per design. He also worked quickly, perpetrating more than 600 courses. However, with the exception of the US Open course at Medinah Country Club in Chicago, most of his work was mediocre. Indeed, his modus operandi was referred to derisively as "18 stakes on a Sunday afternoon".

But the new and better ball commanded new and better courses, so architects took up their T-squares and went back to the drawing board, designing longer layouts and adding thousands of yards to those that existed.

In Pittsburgh, Henry and William Fownes unveiled Oakmont, an extreme test of golf with long, narrow fairways, more than 200 bunkers and 18 fiercely sloped greens that were maintained at breakneck speed. Their philosophy was simple and stern: "a shot poorly played should be a shot irrevocably lost". With Oakmont, the penal school of golf course architecture was born and a wave of defiant American courses would follow.

Meanwhile, golf's first top-notch resort course began to take shape when in 1901 Donald Ross emigrated from the links of Royal Dornoch in Northern Scotland to the sandhills of North Carolina and started work on his masterpiece, Pinehurst Number 2.

At the same time, a Philadelphia hotel owner named George Crump became obsessed with

• Above
George Crump sought to design the world's hardest golf course and did just that at Pine Valley.

constructing the hardest golf course in the world. With the assistance of English architect Harry Colt, he did just that in the pine barrens of southern New Jersey with the creation of Pine Valley. Every fairway and green on the course was set off by the sand and scrub that characterised the region. As such it was a relentless island-to-island examination in shot making and strategy. When Pine Valley opened in 1913 other designers, including Donald Ross and CB Macdonald, hailed it as the finest course in America, and astoundingly, it has remained that way. In the most recent update of Golf Magazine's "100 Best Courses in the World," Pine Valley ranks number one.

Three more Philadelphians would leave indelible marks on golf course design. Albert Tillinghast worked his magic mostly in the East, with Winged Foot and Baltusrol his lasting monuments. George Thomas migrated to Southern California to design a pair of gems at Riviera and the Los Angeles Country Club. And Hugh Wilson stayed home, crafting a masterpiece at Merion.

From the beginning, these courses were more playable and enjoyable than their predecessors – not because of their design, but because of the advent in 1913 of the power mower. Suddenly, fairways and greens could be maintained swiftly and meticulously. Even at the Old Course in St Andrews, the trusty four-legged agronomists were at last relieved of their duties. Golf would never be the same again.

• Above
George Crump with his epic creation, rated one of the best golf courses in the world.

• Above
George Crump, developer and architect.

The Great Triumvirate

Chapter FOUR

Harry Vardon

To many golfers, the name Vardon describes the grip they use to apply their hands to the golf club, whereby the little finger of the right hand rides piggyback on the forefinger of the left hand. Or perhaps to followers of the American professional golf scene it rings a bell as the name on the trophy for the tour's leading player in the stroke averages every season. While both such examples are correct, it misses the point somewhat.

For if you place the christian name of Harry in front of this famous surname, you have one of the most influential characters who ever played the game. And not just because he did indeed lend his name to the most popular grip in golf and latterly a trophy in the United States. Harry Vardon's name means more than any swing technique or silverware ever could. He was a golfing pioneer in every sense of the word and his influence was almost revolutionary.

Our only visual references for Vardon are lifeless, black-and-white photographs – a man who seemingly hit golf shots in between puffs on his pipe – which cannot even begin to convey what a wonderful golfer and charismatic figure he was. Born in Jersey in 1870, Vardon started caddying at a young age and was utterly smitten by golf the very first time he set eyes on the game. He was precociously gifted and, although it was actually his elder brother who turned professional first, Harry had his mind set and soon followed in the footsteps of his sibling. Moreover, he quickly established himself as the superior golfer of the two.

By the time he was in his early 20s, this softly-spoken, elegant swinger was playing a game like no other golfer. He could fade it, draw it, knock it down or loft it up, but most of all he could hit it straight – very straight. Vardon, they say, was unable to play 36 holes on the same day at the same course because, in the afternoon, he'd have to hit his approach shots out of the divots he'd taken in the morning!

Vardon's game was indeed all about precision and placement. He was a slimly-built fellow, and not a particularly healthy specimen at that, suffering as he did from illness for much of his playing career. He did not have the physical presence to overpower a golf course, but that didn't matter. He knew how to

• Above left
Although Harry Vardon wasn't the first to use the overlapping grip which bore his name, he was responsible for popularising it.

• Above right
Vardon's strength was in the power and accuracy of his swing.

by which time he was suffering from what would now be considered the 'yips'. Not that he let it stop him winning tournaments and major championships; Vardon's determination and grit were easily the match of his physical skills. At the 1914 Open, the last to be contested before the Great War intervened, Vardon proved he had longevity to go with all the rest of his considerable talents by winning the championship at the age of 44 years and 42 days, the oldest man to do so since Old Tom Morris in 1867. And Old Tom's victory was during the Open's previous incarnation, when a belt was the prize and the fields were considerably smaller. Roberto de Vicenzo, victor at Hoylake in 1967, is the only man to win an Open in its present format at an older age than Vardon – and then by only 51 days.

Vardon's career had a multitude of highlights, but the 1900 US Open was especially significant, a defining moment in fact. Having made the arduous and time-consuming journey across the Atlantic by boat to play in this event, only recently extended to 72 holes, he arrived at the Chicago Golf Club basically at the peak of his powers. Already he had three Open Championships to his credit and there would be three more to come over the next 14 years. But this was his opportunity to make his mark in front of a new audience. And he seized it with both hands...presumably using a Vardon grip.

He won that US Open with a display of patient, precision golf that lent something of an inevitable air to his game. It was a characteristic of Vardon's golf that opponents would find unnerving, at times dispiriting. Vardon had a quiet, inner confidence. He wasn't one for animated gestures, he certainly wasn't one to shout about his talents. But in the shape of his golf shots Vardon's gifts were there for all to see. And in his prime, mentally he was unshakeable. He was, without a shadow of a doubt, the best golfer in the world at that time.

He later went on to play in two more US Opens

break down its defences with equally effective weapons such as guile and skill. Driving the ball as straight as he did meant he was more often than not playing shots from the fairway, and he capitalised on this by becoming one of the great iron players of his generation, striking the ball crisply and with great accuracy.

He was a fine putter, but only until his late 30s,

• Above
Vardon was the first Englishman to win the Open. He went on to record an unbeaten six victories.

during subsequent tours of America in which he would play exhibition matches, and he finished second on both occasions. The second of those runner-up spots was as a 50-year-old man, not in good health at all, but still talented enough to hold a four-shot lead with seven holes to play. In his heyday, it would have been unthinkable that Vardon would let the title slip through his fingers. But he was considerably weakened by his illness and that ultimately proved his undoing. His major winning days were over, but what a time he'd had of it.

• Above
Born in Earlsferry, Scotland, James Braid (1870–1950) is remembered as one of golf's great champions.

• Inset
Braid instructing customers at Harrods on the basics of the game, 1914.

James Braid

During Vardon's exceptional playing career, there were really only two players in Britain who could give the great man more than a decent game. They even had the talent to beat him. These two men consisted of a fellow Englishman, the sturdy JH Taylor and a bushy-moustached Scotsman, James Braid. For the best part of 20 years the three of them dominated the game and collectively they rightly became known as 'The Great Triumvirate'.

James Braid was tall and powerful, a colourful character whose popularity and supreme talents never deserted him all the time he was involved in the game. He was an awesome hitter in his day, with big hands and an aggressive golf swing ideally suited to the task of smashing the ball as far as possible. He wasn't the straightest of hitters, but that didn't concern him. In all truth it wasn't even a problem, because allied to that great power Braid had a very fine touch around the greens. Throughout his career he possessed a terrific short game and his powers of recovery were as legendary as his powers off the tee.

Born just down the road from the Home of Golf at St Andrews, one would have assumed that this might give young Braid something of a kick-start in the game, but he was from a poor family and golf did not find him easily. However, once Braid and golf got together it was an ideal match. He soon developed into a fine player, although he was slow to make a name for himself and of the three members of the Great Triumvirate he was the last to hit the big time.

Mind you, it was always merely a question of

'when' and not 'if' he would become a champion. And while you might say Braid took his time establishing himself as a major force, he soon won major trophies like a man in an awful hurry. Witness his Open record. Before Braid had won even his first Open Championship, Harry Vardon had three to his name. And yet Braid was the first man to win five Opens, a record he compiled in an extraordinary 10-year spell of golf. He wasn't fussy about where he won, either. Two of his championships were won at Muirfield, one at Prestwick, and another two on his home patch at St Andrews.

Braid was a wonderfully exciting golfer to watch. Outwardly he maintained a calm demeanour, but his golf was considerably more animated. You might say he played the game in the same flamboyant, attacking style as that which Arnold Palmer employed to such devastating effect some 50 years later and Seve Ballesteros subsequently also embraced. It made him popular with galleries, who relished the fact that with Braid one never quite knew what was coming next, but it was invariably worth watching nonetheless.

While still every bit the champion golfer, he had the foresight or good fortune (perhaps a bit of both), to land the job as the first club professional at the lovely Walton Heath Golf Club in Surrey. Whether or not he knew it at the time, it proved to be a very good move. He was popular with the members and enjoyed the good life, as he richly deserved.

He also made quite a name for himself in golf course architecture and was a prolific designer, undoubtedly more so than the other two members of the Great Triumvirate. Braid was responsible for literally dozens of golf courses all over Britain and his legacy lives on in such classic layouts as the fabulous King's Course at Gleneagles, the rugged St Enedoc in Cornwall, the beautiful Blairgowrie Rosemount course in Scotland and the delightful Luffenham Heath in Rutland, plus far too many others to mention.

• Above pictures
Braid won his first Open in 1901 and within ten years he became the first man to win the event five times.

• Below
Braid was a prolific golf course designer with his legend living on in great layouts including the King's Course at Gleneagles.

JH Taylor

The final member of the Great Triumvirate was JH Taylor. Before James Braid came on to the scene, Taylor was Vardon's greatest rival. Indeed, he was something of a young prodigy, winning a couple of Open Championships before Vardon had even opened his account. Taylor didn't get things all his own way for long, though. He and Vardon, along with Braid, were involved in some classic championship duels, from which they would each claim their share of triumphs.

Like Braid, Taylor grew up playing golf by the seaside, not in Scotland but on the wonderful links of Westward Ho! in Devon. Despite this similarity in their golfing upbringing, Taylor's game could scarcely have been further removed from that of Braid. While the Scotsman had a huge, powerful golf swing which produced towering drives, Taylor had a tidy, compact swing which meant his speciality was crafting low, punchy iron shots. No other golfer of that time struck the ball with quite the same authority. He was a sturdy fellow, with a low centre of gravity and excellent balance. All in all, he had every quality you could possibly wish for in order to play great golf in windy conditions.

As a result, his game was made for championship golf and, not surprisingly, Taylor thrived on the windswept links courses on which the Open Championship has always been played. And to go with his wonderful all-round game Taylor had the ideal temperament, as do all the great champions. He could remain calm at times when other golfers became flustered. He could think clearly, which gave him the ability to choose the right shots under pressure. And he knew how to finish the job off, to grasp a winning opportunity whenever it presented itself.

Taylor was so obviously made of the stuff of champions that it was no surprise at all when he

fired a first-round 75 in the 1893 Open Championship at Prestwick, which at the time was a record score. He failed to win the championship that year, but that single supreme round of golf was a taste of things to come.

At the Open the following year, played at Sandwich, he made the big breakthrough by becoming the first Englishman to win the championship, on the first occasion the event had ever been held outside Scotland. When the championship returned home to St Andrews the following year, Taylor won it again. Twelve months later at Muirfield, he was within a whisker of winning it for a third year in a row but, having tied with his great rival Vardon after 72 holes, he lost the two-round playoff. Nevertheless, it was the start of an impressive sequence for Taylor in the Open Championship. He'd acquired the sweet taste for winning and it stayed with him for many years to come.

Perhaps Taylor's finest achievement was at the 1900 Open Championship at St Andrews, where he produced the lowest score in every round on the way to a wire-to-wire victory by an emphatic margin. It was a performance of utter domination, leaving his great rivals Braid and Vardon trailing. That same year he came close in the US Open, but was pipped by, guess who...Harry Vardon.

Like his rivals, Taylor also made a huge contribution to the game aside from his exploits with a club in his hand. He was equally gifted with a pencil and paper, as he designed many fine golf

• Opposite
James Henry Taylor (1871–1963). As well as being a member of The Great Triumvirate, Taylor also founded the PGA.

• Above
JH Taylor won the first of his three Open titles in 1894.

• Above
The Great Triumvirate, JH Taylor, (back right) Harry Vardon, (front right) and James Braid (front left) are joined by 1902 Open champion Alex 'Sandy' Herd.

courses, including his beloved Royal Mid Surrey where he became the pro, and Datchet near Windsor.

More far-reachingly, he helped elevate the status of his fellow professional, much in the way that Henry Cotton would successfully attempt to do some 20 or 30 years later. The doyen of golf writing at that time, Bernard Darwin, who was The Times' correspondent and himself a fine amateur golfer, memorably described Taylor's efforts as "turning a feckless company into a self-respecting and respected body of men."

As far as character references go, it might have been a little harsh on your typical professional golfer! It certainly doesn't quite do the man justice, for Taylor's influence was far-reaching and long-lasting. He was a speaker of high regard, articulate with his words and much in demand for public engagements. His status became such that he alone is regarded as the man most responsible for setting up the fledgling Professional Golfers Association, which today is still charged with looking after the interests of its members.

The Great Triumvirate

If there had ever been such a thing as a winner's podium for the top-three finishers in major championships during the latter half of the 19th century and the beginning of the 20th, the sight of Vardon, Braid and Taylor occupying all three positions would have been a familiar scenario. The combined records of this Great Triumvirate are simply astonishing. Even if there are some detractors who might be churlish enough to say that by today's standards far fewer golfers were competing in championships during that era, it cannot in any way lessen the magnitude of their on-course efforts.

Between 1894 and 1914, Braid, Taylor and Vardon won 16 of the 21 Open Championships, and in each of the five years when another man won, one of these three finished second. By the time their winning ways were over, Braid and Taylor had five championships each to their name, and Vardon had six – a landmark which to this day has never been matched, let alone surpassed. It may never be, not even by Tiger Woods.

Vardon is rightly judged one of the greatest of the great, but these impressive statistics are not the only meaningful benchmark. His success had numerous effects on the game, not least of which was the transformation of the golf swing and how it was taught.

At the end of the 19th century, a heated debate pitted the proponents of the flat, around-the-body St Andrews swing against a new motion, better suited to the gutta-percha ball, which had recently been introduced. The technique may also have evolved from the open stance (body aiming slightly left of the target) employed by those adherents to the object of Britain's other great sporting fanaticism, cricket.

Not only did cricketers stand open, but they employed a great deal of wrist action and made contact slightly on the upswing (rather than on the downswing as the St Andreans did, the result of playing the ball so far back in the stance). But the most important difference was the path of the swing, which, rather than rotating flatly around the torso, went up above the shoulders with the club extending to head-height. The result of all these actions was a ball that was lofted high into the air – heresy to the traditionalists who fervently believed in the low-flying projectiles of Old and Young Tom.

But the diehards' cause was soon dead and buried. In 1890 Englishman John Ball won both the British Amateur and Open Championship with an upright swing. Four years later, Taylor briefly stemmed the tide by winning his first Open by addressing the ball from an open stance and using a cricketer's motion. Then along came Vardon, whose successes were successive nails in the coffin of the St Andrews swing.

Not only did Vardon use an upright swing, he wrote about it. While not the first golf-instruction author, Vardon was one of the first to produce best-sellers in which he described his methods in intricate detail. Here is an excerpt from The Complete Golfer, first published in 1905:

"'Slow back' is a golfing maxim that is both old and wise. The club should begin to gain speed when the upward swing is about half made, and the increase should be gradual until the top is reached, but it should never be so fast that control of the club is to any extent lost at the turning point. The head of the club should be taken back fairly straight from the ball…for the first six inches, and after that any tendency to sweep it round sharply to the back should be avoided. Keep it very close to the straight line until it is halfway up. The old St Andrews style of driving largely consisted of this sudden sweep round, but the modern method appears to be easier and productive of better results."

And this is but a fraction of his comments just on driving. There were separate chapters on the brassie

• Above
Vardon's upright swing and his great success spelt the end for the wristy St Andrews swing.

• Above
The ultimate gutty was the Vardon Flyer, which Harry promoted on a tour of the US.

and the spoon, the cleek, mid-irons, the mashie, bunker play and putting, as well as sections on competitive play, caddies, golf for ladies and on his favourite courses, plus a few chapters of autobiography. By 1921, The Complete Golfer (perhaps the most accurately titled golf book of all time) had gone through 17 sold-out editions.

With Vardon at the lead, closely followed by Taylor, Braid and the other great British players, the new upright swing took hold. In the United States it was championed by HJ Whigham, a Scotsman who had been educated at Oxford, emigrated to Chicago, won back-to-back US Amateurs, and wooed and married the great CB Macdonald's daughter.

He then wrote How To Play Golf, America's first great instruction book, which was published in 1897, one year after Vardon's first Open Championship victory. Whigham was heavily influenced by Vardon's swing, and wrote in his book, "Don't, above all, as you value your golfing future, adopt a full St Andrews swing… It is better to miss the ball in the right way than to hit it in the wrong." Quite a compliment, as it happens.

Along with his influence on the swing, Vardon had a profound effect on golf commerce. His visit to America in 1900 wasn't solely to play in the fledgling US Open, but was part of golf's first big endorsement contract: equipment maker AG Spalding paid Vardon £900 (a considerable amount of money, seeing as at that time the prize for winning the Open Championship was a mere £30) to make a nine-month-long publicity tour of the States to promote the company's hot new gutty ball, the Vardon Flyer. Around that time, he became almost certainly the first golfer to endorse a non-golfing product when he was paid to promote the merits of a plaster designed for aches and sprains. For one who didn't enjoy the best of health, it was entirely appropriate!

For a nation newly hooked on golf, Vardon's visit was mesmerising. Wherever he went, hundreds of people came to see him, even in steely New York City, where Vardonmania was so fervent that on the day of his visit the Stock Exchange closed down. Vardon was initially amazed at the reception he received and how much the fans seemed to adore him. But he would soon get used to it, not just in tournaments where his shins and ankles would often be bruised from being kicked by spectators as they rushed to see his shots, but anywhere he chose to wield a golf club. They wanted to see just how well a golf ball could be struck.

And Vardon, not one to disappoint an audience, showed them. His skills with a golf club had audiences simply spellbound. During one exhibition at a Boston department store, when he became bored hitting shot after shot into a net, he spotted a sprinkler valve protruding through the net and amused himself, and most people watching, by aiming for it. He hit the valve so many times that the store manager begged him to stop for fear of flooding the store.

Vardon played more than 70 matches on his tour, winning all but about a dozen of them, a remarkable record considering he was travelling vast distances by train, playing courses he'd never seen before, and, more often than not, matching his score against

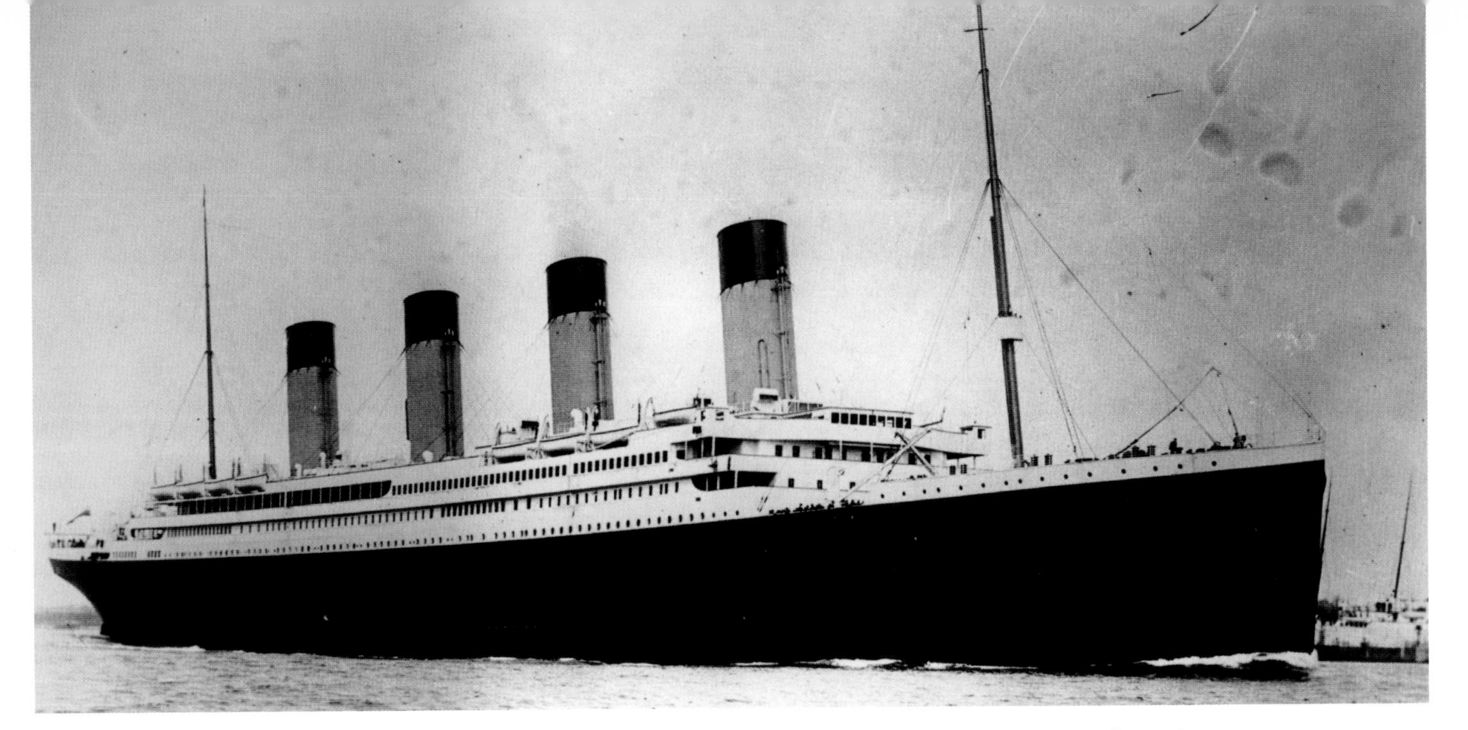

the better ball of two local opponents. Thousands of people would turn up to watch Vardon's exhibition matches, revelling in an almost carnival-like atmosphere as a band would play leading up to the tee-off times.

In June, Harry hopped back across the Atlantic for the Open Championship at St Andrews where he finished second as Taylor won and Braid placed third. Then, as we covered a little earlier in this chapter, he returned by boat to America and capped his triumphant tour in Chicago with a victory in the US Open, turning the tables on Taylor, who finished second by two strokes.

There was nothing fortunate about Vardon's golf, but there may have been some good fortune in the timing of some of his travel arrangements. He was due to travel to the States in 1912 for the US Open, but was forced to cancel when illness again made it impossible for him to make the arduous journey by sea. It meant he had to cancel a reservation on the maiden voyage of a certain boat...called the Titanic.

Vardon's performances in the Open Championship had well and truly cemented his place in history. But it is a measure of the man's greatness that he had by then made an equally huge impression on the other side of the Atlantic. Vardon's amazing grace transformed the curious into converts, and golf in America began a big-time boom. Before Vardon arrived, golf was almost a novelty. By the time he'd made his mark, it had become a passion. By the end of 1900 there was at least one golf course in every state – a thousand courses in all – and the US boasted a quarter of a million players, more than the rest of the world combined.

Vardon's presence is felt even today. Like the other two members of the Great Triumvirate he is responsible for some of his country's finest golf courses, including the gem that is Little Aston in Staffordshire and, among the many others which carry his name, South Herts, the club just north of London to which he was attached when he won his last three Open Championships.

The grip he popularised is rightly named after him, as is the trophy for the leading professional each year on the US Tour stroke averages. There is a poetic justice in the fact that a trophy bearing Vardon's name should be contested by golfers adept at low scoring over a sustained period, because that was one of his specialities. In his day, nobody did it better.

The First World War effectively signalled the end of the Great Triumvirate's reign for, when championship golf was put back on the calendar, Vardon, Taylor and Braid were all pretty much past their best. The game of golf got seriously lucky, though, because as they stepped aside so three great young American golfers moved on to the scene.

Enter Walter Hagen, Bobby Jones and Gene Sarazen. A new triumvirate was born. Incredibly, their collective brilliance would set alight the golfing world just as brightly as the previous generation and be equally as influential both on and off the golf course. Golf was lucky indeed.

• ***Above***
Due to illness Vardon was forced to cancel his berth on board the ill-fated Titanic.

The Ultimate Amateur

Chapter FIVE

5

Bobby Jones

He was only 14 years old when he burst upon the American scene in the 1916 US Amateur at Merion, but even then the name Robert Tyre Jones Jnr was well known throughout his native Georgia. A year earlier he had shot a course-record 68 at his home club – the East Lake Country Club in Atlanta – where he had been the club champion at age 12. Then, just two weeks before heading north, he had beaten a field full of men twice his age to become the Georgia State Amateur Champion. Bobby Jones was a certified prodigy.

At Merion, Jones made his way through two matches before losing to the defending champion, Bob Gardner, while captivating everyone with his long drives, crisp irons and fearless assault on the course. Even the hard-bitten old campaigner Walter Travis was impressed. When asked how much room for improvement the young lad had, Travis stroked his white beard and said "Improvement? He can never improve on his shots, if that's what you mean. But he will learn a great deal more about playing them."

In those days, Jones's only weakness was a terrible temper. He was prone to fits of extreme anger, cursed like a dock worker and threw clubs at the smallest provocation. In time, however, he learned to control his competitive fire, and there then flourished one of the grandest careers in the history of sport.

The Ultimate Amateur

Within a period of eight years, from 1923 to 1930, Jones won four US Opens, three British Opens, five US Amateurs, and one British Amateur – a total of 13 national championships, 62 per cent of those he entered. Of his last 12 Opens – nine in the US and three in Britain – he won seven, and in four of the other five he was runner-up. No player before or since has come close to matching such a phenomenal record.

What is all the more astounding is that Jones compiled that record while playing no more golf than the average duffer. An amateur to the core, he put his family first, then his business as a lawyer, and finally golf. He hated practice, going months at a time without picking up a club, and in some years the only tournaments he played were the national championships he won.

Bobby Jones was a supremely natural player, a golf genius. While others, even some of the best players, hit doggedly at the ball, Jones swept serenely through it with a broad, rhythmic swing whose lazy grace belied its power.

He was not a big man – just 5ft 9in and 12½ stone – but he was among the longest hitters of his time. His tee shots averaged 250 yards – with a hickory-shafted driver – and for decades he was the only man ever to get home in two at the 17th hole of the Olympic Club in San Francisco, a par five of 603 yards. But Jones's true strengths were his surgically accurate irons and his touch with Calamity Jane, the simple blade putter he used throughout his career.

Jones had already established himself as the best golfer in the world when, in 1930, he did the unthinkable. He won the Open and Amateur titles of America and Great Britain, all four national championships, in the span of one astonishing season, a feat The New York Sun christened "the impregnable quadrilateral". Ever since, it has been known as golf's 'Grand Slam'. More than 70 years

• Above
Young Bobby Jones at the 1921 British Amateur Championships at Hoylake.

• Inset
Jones with his wife in 1926.

later it still remains the most extraordinary achievement in the history of the game.

It was a journey that stretched across four months and several thousand miles, beginning in St Andrews, Scotland, with the title Jones most wanted to win, the British Amateur. Victory here involved a gruelling series of eight matches, and the path wasn't easy, as in three of those encounters Bobby squeezed through by the narrowest 1-up margin. In the 36-hole final against England's finest player, Roger Wethered, brother of Joyce and winner of the 1923 British Amateur, Jones won by a convincing seven holes up with six to play.

Two weeks later, at Hoylake, Jones took the lead after 36 holes, broke the competitive course record for 72 and won his third British Open by two strokes over Leo Diegel and Macdonald Smith. No American had ever won both of these titles, back to back or otherwise, and on his return to the States, New Yorkers gave their conquering hero a ticker-tape parade.

Then he was off to Minnesota and the US Open at Interlachen Country Club, where a 68 in round three put him in what seemed to be the driver's seat with a five-stroke lead. In the final round, however, Jones double-bogeyed three of the four par–3 holes, allowing Mac Smith to give chase again. But, in a display of the competitive resilience that was his trademark, Jones finished with birdies on three of his last six holes for a two-stoke victory. The clincher was a dramatic 40-footer at the 72nd green.

By this time a victory in the final leg, the US Amateur, seemed pre-ordained, especially since the tournament had returned to Merion, the site of Jones's national championship debut. And that is exactly the way it turned out. Bobby won the qualifying medal for lowest score, was never down to an opponent in any of his matches and, in the

• ***Above***
Jones with the Open trophy, US Open trophy, US Amateur trophy and the Walker Cup.

36-hole final, beat Eugene Homans by a score of eight up with seven holes to play.

On that day, a unit of 50 US Marines in full dress was assigned to escort Jones as he played his way through a throng of 18,000 well-wishers, but even the Marines could not suppress the universal joy at Merion's 11th green when Bobby completed his triumphant journey.

Bobby Jones might have been an object of intense envy had he not also been the epitome of modesty and grace. A genuine Southern gentleman, he was highly educated, with degrees in engineering, English literature and law. He not only read books, he wrote them, and he wrote about golf just as gracefully as he played it.

At a time when America led the way with larger-than-life sports heroes – from Babe Ruth and Ty Cobb in baseball to Bill Tilden in tennis and Jack Dempsey in boxing – Bobby was revered above them all. Yet he remained humble, unaffected and unassuming. At Harvard, where he earned his degree in English, Jones was ineligible for the golf team, having already played at his previous university, Georgia Tech. So he served as the team's assistant manager. At the time he was the US Open Champion!

He also was a man of immense integrity. In four different national championships, he called penalties on himself for minor infractions. When he was praised for this, Jones was almost indignant, saying, "There is only one way to play the game. You might as well praise someone for not robbing a bank." Jones's name was so synonymous with perfect behaviour that the USGA named its highest award for sportsmanship after him.

Jones's career was as brief as it was brilliant. When he completed the Grand Slam, he was only 28 – and at that point, having achieved all of his goals and more, and worn himself out in the process, he retired, devoting the remainder of his life to his family and his business.

He had plenty to keep him occupied. He published three books (written with his regular travelling companion, newspaperman OB Keeler), designed a set of golf clubs for Spalding and collaborated with Warner Brothers Studios on a series of instructional film shorts that co-starred the likes of Jimmy Cagney, Edward G Robinson, Loretta Young and WC Fields.

But the lion's share of Jones's energy went into the pursuit of a dream. In June of 1931 that dream began to take shape when he and a group of investors purchased 365 acres of land near the city of Augusta, Georgia. And in January of 1933 it became reality when the Augusta National – Bobby Jones's dream course – opened for play.

It was an unlikely venture at an unlikely time – about 10 years late to be exact. The previous decade or so had been the golden age of American golf course architecture, with more highly regarded courses being built than in any two decades before or since, from Pebble Beach and Cherry Hills in the West to Inverness and Medinah in the middle of the country to Quaker Ridge and Seminole in the East. But 1933 was the middle of the Great Depression in America, a time when golf clubs were closing by the dozen, and that is when Jones chose to unveil his pride and joy.

• ***Above***
Jones (right) with Gene Sarazen, two legends of the game.

The site of the course was equally unlikely – a Civil War indigo plantation that had been bought by a Belgian nobleman and converted into a horticultural nursery called Fruitlands. The rolling countryside was planted with a dazzling assortment of trees, shrubs and flowers, with Georgia pines, azaleas and dogwoods prominent throughout.

Alister Mackenzie, the famed Scottish architect, agreed to collaborate with Jones on the design of the course. A medical graduate from Cambridge University, Mackenzie had served in the Boer War as a field surgeon before a falling-out with the British Army. A proficient artist and writer, his 1920 treatise on the subject, 'Golf Architecture', is still the clearest and most concise exposition on the subject, and an avid golfer, he soon turned his attention to golf course design. His first creation was The Alwoodley Golf Course near Leeds, designed in 1907 and officially recognised as one of Britain's finest inland

• **Above**
Jones playing during the 1927 Open where he won his second of three Open titles.

• **Below**
Jones chose Scottish golf course architect Alister Mackenzie as his collaborator on the design of the Augusta National.

courses. He then designed the Moortown Golf Club, also in Leeds, in 1909, a course that went on to stage the Ryder Cup in 1929. An inveterate traveller as well as a prolific designer, Mackenzie's creations include Australia's oldest club, The Royal Melbourne, designed in 1926, and America's Cypress Point in California, a 1928 creation considered, like Royal Melbourne, to be among the top 10 courses in the world.

Jones first played Cypress Point in 1929, a year after it opened. He had travelled to Pebble Beach to compete in the US Amateur – he was the defending champion – but was knocked out surprisingly in the first round. Rather than leave, he hung around and played Cypress Point a few times; there his admiration for Mackenzie's work was born.

In Augusta, as Mackenzie drew the maps and oversaw the earth-moving, Jones played thousands of experimental shots from planned tees to planned greens. He had two strong desires: first, that the course have a natural look, that it rise out of the terrain rather than be stamped upon it, in a way he hoped would recall the softly rolling feel of the Scottish linksland he so loved; and second, that each hole offer alternative lines of attack, allowing a player to choose among conservative, mildly aggressive and audacious routes from tee to green, with the reward in proportion to the risk.

When the design was finished, Mackenzie called it his finest achievement. Its generous fairways, sparse bunkering and expansive greens gave the Augusta National a wide-open, welcoming appearance. It looked easy, but didn't play that way – and that was exactly what Jones wanted.

"There is not a hole on the course where you can't make birdie if you just think," he said, "but there is not a hole where you won't make bogey if you stop thinking." Today, despite more than 60 changes, the Augusta National remains what Jones envisioned: a masterpiece of strategic design and the quintessential 'thinking man's' golf course.

Jones conceived his course as a retreat where he and his friends could enjoy the game they loved in beautiful surroundings and with a degree of privacy. But almost immediately after the Augusta National opened, the USGA expressed interest in holding a

• ***Above***
Jones's 1930 Grand Slam remains the most impressive achievement in the history of the game.

• Above
Augusta's famous 18th tee shot. Jones's number-one venture was the creation of the Augusta National Golf Course which opened in 1933.

US Open there, the first US Open to be held in the South. The Augusta National members were struck by the idea, but the thought of the USGA or any group moving in to run a tournament on their course did not sit well. "If we're going to hold a tournament," they reasoned, "let's hold our own."

And so in 1934 The Masters was born with Jones as host and his Augusta co-founder, Clifford Roberts, as the tournament chairman. Actually, in those days it was called The Augusta National Invitation, and that's what it was, an invitation from Jones to his old compatriots and the best of the new players, both professional and amateur, to get together for some good golf and good times. But it became something more than that the moment Roberts convinced his partner to play. Once word got out, newspapers from coast to coast headlined the biggest golf news in four years: Bobby Jones is coming out of retirement!

Jones played well from tee to green, but his chipping and putting were not what either he or the public had hoped to see. He opened with a 76 and finished the tournament at 294, in a tie for 13th place, 10 strokes behind winner Horton Smith. That was as well as Bobby would do in any of the dozen Masters in which he played.

In the short time that he was at golf's centre stage, Jones had enraptured golf fans on two continents, but nowhere more than in the city of St Andrews. It was here that so much of his career had unfolded, from his first embarrassing appearance in the Open in 1921, when a stretch of poor play led him to tear up his scorecard and stomp off the course, to the Open he dominated from start to finish in 1927, to his crowning achievement in the Amateur of 1930.

In 1936 he returned to the town, quietly and unannounced, for a casual round of golf. Yet by the time he reached the first tee of the Old Course, 5,000 St Andreans were waiting to see him play. "Our Bobby is back," they rejoiced.

More than 20 years passed before Jones returned again to the 'Old Grey Toun', and when he did it was for one of the most poignant occasions in sport, as he was made a Freeman of the Royal Burgh of St Andrews, the first American so honoured since Ben Franklin in 1757. By this time, at the age of 56, Jones's body had been tragically wracked by a degenerative neuromuscular disease called syringomyelia. He had not played golf in years and could barely stand but, as he accepted his honour, his heart and mind were as strong as ever.

Jones said, "I can take out of my life everything except my experience at St Andrews, and I would still have a rich, full life."

Bobby Jones died in 1971, leaving a legend and a legacy like no other. His longtime friend, sportswriter Grantland Rice, said it best: "Whatever any future giant of the links does to par, no one will ever replace Bobby Jones in the hearts of those to whom golf means more than a game."

Jones's spirit lives on with the annual playing of the Masters, an event that has grown in leaps and bounds since its modest start in 1934. And the biggest leap came just one year after its inception, when one of the game's most popular players, diminutive Gene Sarazen, fired "the shot heard round the world".

Sarazen was three strokes off the lead in the final round when he came to Augusta National's 15th hole, a 500-yard par five with a pond just in front of the green. After a good tee shot left him roughly 230 yards from the hole, he elected to go for the green with a 4-wood. (Sarazen was playing that day with Walter Hagen, who supposedly pressed Gene to hurry up as he didn't want to be late for a date he'd made for that evening.)

In his usual no-nonsense manner, Sarazen planted his feet, positioned his club (closing the face a bit so it would fly longer and lower), and smacked briskly through the ball. It shot out on a low trajectory and straight at the flag, then cleared the pond, took one big bounce and rolled straight into the cup for a 2 – an albatross. Sarazen had made up all three strokes with one glorious shot. He went on to par the last three holes and clinch a tie with Craig Wood. whom he trounced the next day in a 36-hole playoff.

Suddenly, Bobby Jones's tournament had instant tradition and instant panache, and from that point on it has never looked back. Today, The Masters ranks alongside the Open, US Open and the PGA Championship as one of the four most coveted titles in golf.

With his dramatic victory, Sarazen became the first man to win each of those titles, putting the cap on a classic American success story. The son of Italian immigrants, Eugenio Saraceni had learned the game as a caddie in suburban New York, one of the thousands of kids inspired by the heroics of Francis Ouimet. When, at age 15, he saw his name in a newspaper for having made a hole in one, he decided 'Eugenio Saraceni' looked more like the name of a violinist than a golfer, and so he changed it to Gene Sarazen.

Five years later, that name was etched onto the US Open trophy when in 1922 Sarazen won by one stroke over Bobby Jones. Later that same summer he added the PGA title, becoming, at age 20, the youngest champion ever. Then in 1923 he made it two PGAs in a row.

But the success may have been too much too soon, and he fell into a decade of relative decline. As he approached his 30th birthday in 1932, Sarazen analysed his problems and decided his high scores had come largely from one thing: poor play in the bunkers. And so he did something about it, for himself and for the generations of golfers to follow him. He invented the sand wedge.

Sarazen got the idea while flying in a plane with billionaire Howard Hughes. On takeoff, when the tail

• Above
Gene Sarazen from 1932, the year his invention of the sand wedge helped him win the US and British Opens.

fins of the plane went down, the plane rose up. He reasoned that if he could lower the sole of his niblick (9-iron), maybe that would help lift the ball from the sand. So, working in the basement workshop of his Florida home, he soldered a thick flange on the back of the club and angled it so that the flange hit the sand first, allowing the front of the club to bounce upward. Now he could hit behind the ball and splash it out.

Sarazen was not the first to follow this notion. Bobby Jones, Walter Hagen, and Horton Smith all had sought bunker relief with variously doctored niblicks. But Gene was the first to succeed.

Surreptitiously, he brought the club with him to the Open in 1932 at Princes Golf Club, Sandwich, not unveiling it until play began for fear the rules moguls of the Royal & Ancient would ban it. Sarazen's new club worked like a charm, saving him stroke after stroke from the sand while restoring the feisty confidence of his early days. He won the title by five strokes, breaking the 72-hole record in the process. Two weeks later, he won the US Open at Skokie Country Club in a virtuoso performance that saw him cover the final 28 holes in an even 100 strokes – an average of 3.6 strokes per hole.

At about the same time, another major development was occurring on the equipment front. The USGA and the Royal & Ancient had approved the production of golf clubs with shafts made of tubular steel. And this blessing came not a moment too soon, since America's hickory forests had been nearly depleted by the demand for wooden-shafted clubs.

With steel, clubmaking switched from a craft dependent on the skilled eye and hand of an artisan to a purely mechanical process. The most immediate benefit was uniformity: suddenly all clubs were created equal.

Up to this point, golfers had built up their arsenals rather haphazardly, buying a brassie here and a mashie there in hopes of assembling a collection of sticks with similar heft and flex. But, all too often, the result was a bagful of weapons that were eternally at odds with one another. Stiff shafts and whippy shafts, flat lies and upright lies, heavy heads and light heads all came to roost in the same

• Above
Sarazen in action at the Open Championship at Sandwich, 1926.

nest while their bewildered owner wondered how, on a given day, he could be 'on' with one club and 'off' with another.

But steel shafts put an immediate end to that with the advent of the matched set. Not only were the clubs consistent from one to the next, but the lie of the clubhead and the flexibility of the shaft could be custom-tailored to fit individual needs. There was even an ad mentioning a mysterious new measurement called swingweight, the measure of the balance of a club's weight between its grip and head ends, that could be calibrated to a golfer's liking.

It was at this time also that golf clubs began to be designated with numbers instead of names – the spoon became a 3-wood, the mashie a 5-iron, the niblick a 9-iron, and so on – and for a while those numbers got out of hand. With no limit on the number of clubs in a bag, golfers began arriving at the first tee with two dozen and more. Lawson Little, the winner of back-to-back titles in both the US and British Amateurs in 1934 and 1935, is reputed to have secured his quartet of victories with the help of no fewer than 31 clubs.

Clearly, something had to be done, if only to save the sacroiliacs of the caddies, and so in 1938 the USGA put its foot down, limiting the golfer's armaments to 14. The R&A followed a year later, and 14 remains the maximum number to this day.

Four years later another cap was imposed, this time on the liveliness of the golf ball. In the three decades or so since the invention of the Haskell, steady improvements had been made in golf-ball design and production. Back in the 20s, the game's two ruling bodies had limited the size and weight of the ball, but that hadn't stopped one manufacturer from creating a rocket that went 50 yards farther than anything on the market. What's more, as golfers began swinging their steel shafts with a slashing vigour that had been impossible in the hickory era, everyone from tour pros to grandmothers got a jolt of extra distance. So, in 1942, the USGA imposed a limit on the velocity a golf ball may have at impact, namely to 250ft per second when measured under controlled conditions on the Association's testing device.

• Above
Lawson Little practising at Prestwick during the 1934 British Amateur Championship. He went on to win using a reputed 31 clubs.

An American Triumvirate

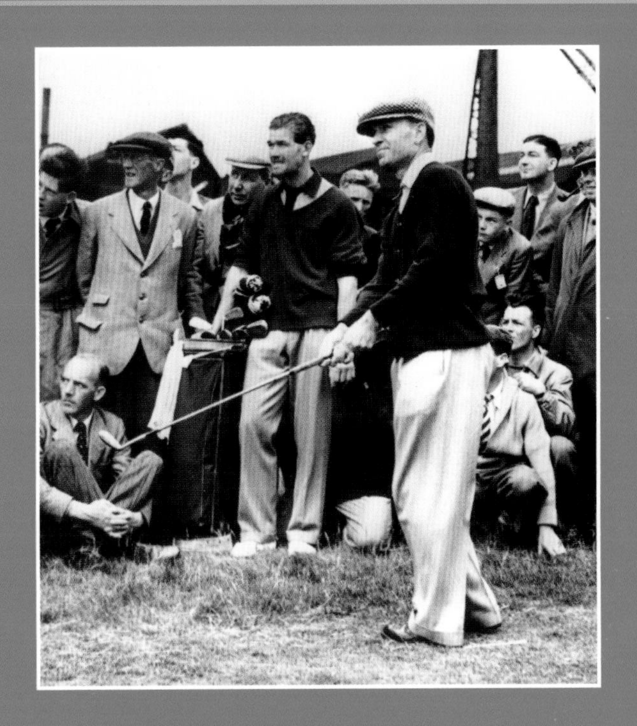

Chapter SIX

An American Triumvirate

As golf equipment became more consistent, more precise, and more powerful, so did golf's best players, and in the late 1930s a new breed of strong and talented professionals came to the fore.

Certainly, the game was in need of them. The retirement of Bobby Jones, combined with the difficulties of the Depression, had thrown big-time golf into a decade of doldrums. Golf historian Herbert Warren Wind captured this pre-War drabness in one picturesque line. "Golf without Jones," he said, "was like France without Paris – leaderless, lightless and lonely." Walter Hagen and Gene Sarazen had done their best to charm the American fans, but their best years had passed. England's answer to Bobby Jones was the legendary Henry Cotton. Some men are born to greatness – at least, so they say. Henry Cotton was surely one of these men. As a young boy he used to autograph pictures of himself, already assuming the status of famous sportsman as if it were the most natural thing in the world to do. And soon, it was.

He discovered golf almost by default, though. Banned by the headmaster from playing cricket at the posh school his wealthy father had sent him to, young Henry responded in a fashion that marked him out as the strong-minded, straight talker he would in later life become, by saying "I'll play golf then, sir."

This, even by the standards of someone who would go on to make a lot of very smart lifestyle choices, was perhaps the smartest of all. Next was his decision as a 20-year-old, and already a professional golfer of considerable talent, to travel to America. He felt that by competing with the best golfers, who at that time were all on the other side of the Atlantic, he'd stand a better chance of becoming the best. Again, he wasn't wrong. He was talented, dedicated, almost obsessive in the way he practised, and it paid off. It gave him the perfect grounding, which served as a springboard to truly great things.

In his prime, Cotton was a sublime ball-striker, at least the equal of legends such as Sam Snead and Ben Hogan. And he was long, exceptionally long, when he needed to be because he was one of those rare golfers who had reserves of effortless power available on tap. This was due in no small part to good technique, but he was also physically very strong – one of his favourite practice drills was standing on a range and hitting 5-iron shots, struck pure and true as the day was long, using just his left arm. Think about that. Left-armed full swings take some doing!

Cotton's golf game oozed class. He drew attention from galleries and fellow players alike. Crowds would love watching him. It didn't matter if he was in contention or not; he was that sort of player. He had a magnetic appeal that only the true greats possess. Players were drawn to him, too, but for different reasons. They felt they could learn

• Opposite
Henry Cotton in full swing.

• Above
Cotton on his way to winning the 1934 Open Championship.

many of whom at that time were treated almost as second-class citizens. It seems ridiculous now, but in that era it was common for them not to be allowed in the clubhouse. Cotton would not stand for such nonsense and was not afraid to say as much.

Ironically, since he did so much to help his fellow professionals, he did not always endear himself to them. In his prime playing days he often preferred not to mix with them, and could seem aloof. And he had a fiery temperament; he managed to learn how to keep it under wraps in order to produce his best golf in championships, but it was often a little bit more in evidence off the golf course. Let's say he was not afraid to call a spade a spade.

But Cotton had a good heart. He could be kind of spirit and generous with his knowledge. In 1938, the year after winning his second Open Championship, he travelled to St Andrews of his own free will and at his own expense, to offer advice and assistance to the members of the Great Britain and Ireland Walker Cup team. Each of the home players was able to tap into Cotton's keen golfing brain, even play a round of golf against him. That year the home side won the Walker Cup for the first time in its history. Cotton's influence had evidently made a difference. But then it always did, whatever company he was keeping and in whatever walk of life. He was not the sort of character who could ever be ignored.

Cotton won three Open Championships in his career. His first win in 1934, at Sandwich, was perhaps his finest. Aged just 27, slimly built and with a somewhat intense and highly strung personality, he'd already finished in the top 10 in his previous

something from studying the great man in action, as if his magic were somehow contagious. In some ways they might have been on to something, because the wonderful rhythm of his swing could easily leave a lasting impression on those who watched, and subconsciously it may have rubbed off.

Cotton was just as influential off the golf course and did much to change the face of professional golf, and how it was perceived. There is no question that he elevated the status of the professional golfer,

• Above

Henry Cotton was a sublime ball-striker and an obsessive practiser.

four Opens. But this time there would be no near miss. From day one Cotton produced world-class golf that literally blew everyone else into the weeds. Starting with a 67, he then shot a 65 in the second round – a championship record score that stood for an incredible 43 years. It was so amazing that it inspired one leading manufacturer to name one of its golf balls in recognition of the achievement; thus the Dunlop 65 was born.

To further put it in perspective, it's worthy of mention that only five golfers broke 70 all week in that Open Championship; Cotton was responsible for two of the rounds and they were back-to-back at the start of the most important tournament of the year. Talk about peaking at the right time! Not surprisingly, it gave him a healthy lead – nine shots, in fact – which proved to be unassailable.

When he won the championship again in 1937, Cotton was at the height of his powers. He would surely have won several more Open titles had the Second World War not then intervened. Circumstance robbed Cotton of his prime competitive years and he had to wait until 1948 to claim his hat-trick. By then he had turned 40 and, while by no means over the hill, was damn near to the top of it. He knew as well as anyone that it would in all likelihood be pretty much downhill soon after that. Mind you, he was still capable of winning tournaments well into the 1950s.

He retired to his beloved Penina golf course in Portugal, where young and ambitious tour pros would flock just to meet the man. Perhaps they hoped, just as the tour pros had who were his contemporaries, that some of the magic might rub off. With Henry, it was always worth a try.

It was across the pond, however, where golf's much-needed shot in the arm was delivered. The professional game needed the boost that a real headliner could provide, and it got not just one but three of them when America produced its own Great Triumvirate: Byron Nelson, Sam Snead, and Ben Hogan.

• *Above*
Henry Cotton holding the Claret Jug after winning his first Open in 1934 at Sandwich.

Byron Nelson

All three were born in the year 1912, but it was Nelson, a lanky, baby-faced Texan, who first gained major attention when he won the 1937 Masters.

He was four strokes off the lead in the final round, and the man in front was Ralph Guldahl, arguably the best player of the time. But, at Augusta's treacherous par-three – 12th hole, Guldahl found water and took a double-bogey 5, then followed with a bogey at the par-five 13th. Nelson, playing just behind him, birdied the 12th and eagled the 13th. Against Guldahl's 5-6 he posted 2-3, picking up six strokes in the space of two holes for a two-stroke lead that he never relinquished.

Two years later, Nelson won the US Open, again in dramatic style, holing a 1-iron approach shot for eagle en route to a playoff victory. That 1-iron, although spectacular, was not unexpected – not from Byron Nelson. For not since Harry Vardon had the game seen anyone hit the ball with the unremitting accuracy of Lord Byron.

His key was his swing – it was a swing unlike all others and was the first swing to adapt successfully to the new and different demands of the steel-shafted club. Nelson, who came to the game as a caddie in Fort Worth, was weaned on hickory, but he came to realise that the 'handsy' style required for

• Pictures
Byron Nelson of the US Ryder Cup team in action at Southport in 1937.

wooden shafts would not work for steel. And so, while the rest of the world continued to imitate Bobby Jones, with little leg movement and a pivot against a tall and braced left side, Nelson put some action in his legs, let his left knee buckle, and actually dipped downward through impact. However, he did continue to use one element of the swing pioneered by Jones – the straight left arm.

Until that time, all the way back to the old St Andreans, the left arm was allowed to bend or 'break down' on the backswing, something players had to do to keep their motion in sync with their wooden-shafted clubs. But suddenly the shafts were firmer, so the leading arm could be, too. Jones was among the first to keep the left arm straight, and it helped him create power, working in conjunction with his straight, strong left side. But if Jones was the first, Nelson was the most important, for along with his other adjustments he helped popularise the 'modern' swing, very similar to the one we use today.

When in form, Byron Nelson simply did not miss shots. And he was in form a good part of the time.

By 1944, Nelson had added a second Masters title, the PGA Championship and two dozen tour victories to his resume. In 1944 alone he won eight events. He had reached a pinnacle few golfers ever know, but he was about to climb much, much higher.

In 1945, Byron Nelson came as close as any golfer has ever come to being unbeatable. There were 35 tournaments on the schedule that year, and Nelson won 18 of them, more than half. Even more incredibly, he won 11 of those events in one

• Above
The great Byron Nelson with the trophy bearing his name.

marvellous, unbroken string. To put that in context, the next longest streak by any man, before or since, is six events.

In addition, Nelson finished second seven times and in 30 events never finished lower than ninth. His total prize money for that year of years was $63,000. The same performance on today's USPGA Tour would earn roughly $20 million.

It has often been argued that this season of dominance could have occurred only at a time when the best of the competition was still away at war. But in fact, Nelson's two main rivals – Hogan and Snead – played in several of those 1945 events. Besides, there was an efficiency about Nelson's performance that year that said nothing and no one could have stopped him. His scoring average for the season was 68.33 – still a record – and for the year he was 320 strokes under par. Indeed, he never failed to finish a tournament that year under par.

At the end of the next season, Nelson followed in the footsteps of Bobby Jones. Exhausted by the grind and with most of his ambitions fulfilled, he retired and followed another dream, using the money he had saved to buy the 800-acre Texas cattle ranch he had always wanted. In fact, along the way, whenever he would earn a good cheque he'd joke, "That's another cow," or "That's the tractor I wanted."

Years later, he returned to the game as a television commentator and as annual host of a tournament in his name. The Byron Nelson Classic, held in a suburb of Dallas, not far from his home town of Fort Worth, is the only PGA Tour event named in honour of a player, and that is altogether fitting, because golf never produced a finer gentleman.

• Above
Sam Snead and Byron Nelson on the first day of the 2001 Masters.

• Inset
Tiger Woods shakes Nelson's hand during the final round of the 2002 Verizon Byron Nelson Classic.

Samuel Snead

Nelson retired in 1946 at the age of 34. At that point, Samuel Jackson Snead was just getting warmed up. Although by 1945 he had three dozen victories under his belt, there were nearly 50 more wins ahead of him in a career that would last another 34 years and beyond.

Slammin' Sam, as he became known, had come out of the backwoods of western Virginia, with more raw talent than the game had ever seen. Although completely self-taught, playing in bare feet with clubs home-made from tree branches, Snead was blessed with a swing as strong and graceful as the leap of a panther.

In his first pro event, the 1936 Hershey Open, Sam stepped to the tee, reared back, and belted his opening drive out of bounds. He teed a second ball and hit it out of bounds, too. For his third attempt, he settled himself, let his swing flow, and drove the green, 350 yards away. With that shot, he had arrived.

Snead finished fifth in that tournament and later that year won his first event. The next year he won five more, the first instalments in an eventual total of 84 victories, more than any man in history.

But in that same 1937 season, Snead also set a pattern of frustration when he finished second in the US Open despite a closing-round 71 and a four-round total of 283, just one stroke off the tournament record at that time. Indeed, the single blemish on his magnificent career is his failure to win the US Open, despite 37 tries, a dozen top-ten finishes, and an agonising four times as runner-up. Here's a big 'if', but a tantalising one: if Sam Snead had managed to shoot 69 in the final round of each US Open in which he was in contention, he would have won five times and reached a playoff in three

• ***Above***
Slammin' Sam Snead's career total of 84 victories is the all-time USPGA Tour record.

other years.

Snead's most painful loss was to Byron Nelson in 1939 at the Spring Mill Country Club near Philadelphia, where a par five on his final hole would have taken the title. Instead, thinking he needed to birdie the hole, Snead stumbled to an inglorious eight that featured three shots from bunkers (only two got out) and a three-putt from 40ft away. "That night I was ready to go out with a gun and pay somebody to shoot me," he said later. "It weighed on my mind so much that I dropped 10 pounds, lost more hair, and began to choke even in practice rounds. My doctor said I was headed for a nervous breakdown."

He had another chance in 1947 at St Louis Country Club, where he holed an eighteen-foot putt on the final green to force a playoff with Lew Worsham. When the two came to the 18th green the next day, still even, both balls were about 30in from the cup. Snead set up to putt first, but Worsham asked for a ruling to determine the order. "That kind of rattled me," Snead said. "But it was a little-bitty downhill putt with a left-to-right break. Yikes! Just the kind of putt that scared the daylights out of me." Snead was, indeed, farther away, and when he finally putted, he missed. Worsham made, for a one-stroke win.

In 1949, at Medinah, Snead needed pars on the last two holes but took three strokes from the edge of the 17th and lost by one to Cary Middlecoff. And in 1953 at Oakmont, he entered the final round just one shot behind Hogan; a final-round 76 left him six back.

But history shows that Snead recovered both his

• Above
Sam Snead practising in 1956 while his son looks on.

composure and his game. No entry in the record book is longer than the one with his name on it: among his seven dozen wins are three Masters, three PGAs, and the 1946 Open from St Andrews by an impressive four strokes, plus scores of lesser titles both at home and abroad. Some counts put the grand total at over 160 victories.

Sam Snead was the Methuselah of the fairways. Age never seemed to slow him. He won at least one tournament in every year until 1962, a quarter-century after he began, and in 1965 he won the Greater Greensboro – his sixth victory in that event – becoming, at the age of 52 years and 10 months, the oldest player ever to win on the USPGA Tour. Nine years later, he came within two strokes of winning again, at Los Angeles, and also tied for third in the 1974 USPGA Championship – at the age of 62!

But even then his competitive days were far from over. In 1979, with consecutive rounds of 67 and 66 in the Quad Cities Open, Snead shot and then bettered his age, the first and only man to perform such feats in USPGA Tour competition. And when in

• ***Above***
Sam Snead playing during the 1937 Open at Carnoustie.

• ***Inset***
Snead with the Claret Jug having won the 1946 Open at St Andrews.

• **Above**
Sam Snead walks across St Andrews' famous Swilken Bridge during the Past Champions Challenge at the 2000 Open Golf Championship.

• **Below**
Sam Snead's incredible career lasted over 40 years.

1980 he won the Commemorative, a Senior event, he became the first golfer to record victories in six different decades. He will likely be the last – despite Gary Player's recent efforts – for Sam Snead surely was one of a kind.

Ben Hogan

While Snead played magnificent golf naturally, Ben Hogan had to, in his own words, "dig it out of the dirt". Just 5ft 8½in tall and weighing under 10 stone, Hogan was the runt of the caddie pen at the Glen Garden Country Club near Fort Worth: coincidentally the same club where Byron Nelson caddied and learned the game. In fact in 1927, Hogan lost the caddie championship to Nelson in a playoff. It was Bantam Ben's first taste of defeat, something he definitely did not enjoy.

But there was more frustration to come for Ben Hogan. For the first several years of his career he, like Nelson and many other players before him,

fought a vicious hook, and had a hard time taming it. He made three abortive attempts at the pro circuit before achieving modest success in 1937. It was another three years – and several near-misses – before he broke through with his first victory at the Pinehurst North-South in 1940. By that time, Nelson and Snead had won 30 tournaments between them.

But Hogan was about to make up for lost time. He won in each of the two weeks following Pinehurst, taking four tournaments in all, and finished the season as the leading money winner. In 1941 and 1942 he continued the domination, piling up a dozen more victories while topping the money list in both years.

Then, just as his game was reaching its peak, Hogan was called to war. He served for two years in the Army Air Corps before his discharge in the late summer of 1945. Once back, he wasted no time, winning five events by the end of the year. Then, in 1946, he put together a season that was nearly as overpowering as Nelson's the year before: of the 32 events he entered, Hogan won 13, finished second in six, and finished third in three while competing weekly against full fields of the game's very best.

Among the tournaments he won was his first major championship – the USPGA – and among those he almost won were The Masters and the US Open. In both of those two, a missed putt at the final hole had cost him a shot at the title.

Hogan didn't much like putting. He saw it as a game within the game of golf, a game he was never remotely able to master. But he came about as close as anyone to mastering golf from tee to green, thanks to a monkish devotion to hard work.

He claimed he preferred practice to play. Four-hour sessions on the range were not unusual for him. Once, when he noticed his fairway woods lost some accuracy when he tired, he deliberately fatigued himself on the practice ground in order to ponder his condition and rectify it. It was through his relentless pursuit of improvement that he banished his unruly hook in favour of a fade, with a safer and softer left-to-right arc that found the fairways and held the greens.

Having discovered this method, he worked at

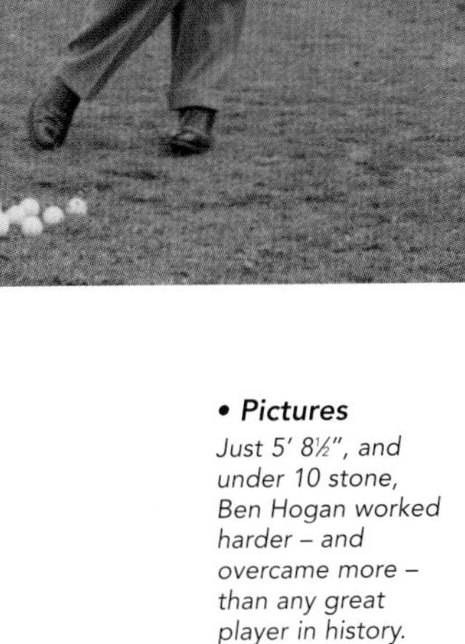

• Pictures
Just 5' 8½", and under 10 stone, Ben Hogan worked harder – and overcame more – than any great player in history.

making it an ingrained part of his game, hitting ball after ball until his swing repeated so automatically that one writer likened it to a machine stamping out bottle tops.

Along with the game's best work ethic, Hogan brought to golf the mind of a championship chess player. On the course he was all concentration, never smiling, almost never speaking. "Eighty per cent of winning is management," he said, and he managed himself and the golf course with a ruthless rigour. His nicknames said it all: he was 'The Hawk' in America, the 'Wee Ice Mon' in Britain.

In 1947, Hogan again led the Tour in victories with seven, and in 1948 he added 10 more, including a second USPGA Championship and his first US Open, won by a commanding five strokes at the Riviera Country Club in Los Angeles.

Eight months later, he was lucky to be alive. In February, after winning two of the first four events on the 1949 Tour, Hogan and his wife Valerie were driving home to Fort Worth when his car collided head-on with a Greyhound bus that had tried to pass a truck on a foggy stretch of Texas highway. Had Hogan not instinctively flung himself in front of his wife to protect her, the steering wheel would have impaled him against the front seat. Instead, he broke his collarbone, fractured his pelvis, crushed his ankle and suffered massive internal injuries.

Doctors said he might never walk again, much less play golf, and it was two months before he was brought home from hospital, weighing under seven stone. But Hogan's will to win was undiminished, and he methodically drilled his body back into shape. By August he was swinging a club and by December he was on the course. The following January he returned to the site of his US Open victory, Riviera, for a comeback. Walking on legs wrapped in elastic bandages from ankle to hip to aid circulation, he shot rounds of 73-69-69-69, and, incredibly, appeared to have won the tournament before

Sam Snead tied him and then prevailed in a playoff.

But Hogan was back, and if any doubters remained he convinced them that June when the US Open came to Merion. Although visibly in pain from the stress of walking a 36-hole final day, he managed to tie Lloyd Mangrum and George Fazio in regulation play, then beat them both the next day in an 18-hole playoff. His victory remains one of the most courageous performances in sport.

Thereafter, Hogan concentrated his limited strength on the major championships, winning his first Masters in 1951 and in the same year taking the US Open title at Oakland Hills near Detroit with a final-round 67 over a course set-up that is still considered the most severe test ever given to the pros.

But Hogan's vintage year was 1953, a season in which he won the Masters, the US Open and the British Open in a span of 12 weeks. At Augusta, he beat Sam Snead by six strokes with a 284 total that lowered the tournament record by five. At Oakmont, he opened with a 67 and led from wire to wire, taking the US Open for the fourth time in his last five starts. Then, persuaded to play the Open for the first time, he sailed across the Atlantic, spent a week learning the subtleties of linksland golf, and assaulted the course and the field at Carnoustie, playing the most gratifying golf of his life. With a course-record 68 in the final round he won by four strokes.

Hogan became only the third player to win the US and British Opens in the same year, and the first to combine them with a victory in the Masters. On his return to the States he became the first golfer since Bobby Jones to get a ticker-tape parade. No player since has been so honoured.

In all, Hogan won nine major championships, six of them in the years following his accident. For golfers everywhere, his name remains a symbol of courage, dedication and indomitable spirit.

And for many it also means hope – hope of improving their own swing. Even though other professionals had written books and magazine articles passing on their magic methods, it was Hogan everyone wanted to hear from. For years, there were rumours of a 'secret', something he had learned during his hours on the practice range.

• Opposite
Ben Hogan plays a tee shot during the fourth annual International Golf Contest for the Canada Cup at Wentworth in 1956. The team event was won by Hogan and Sam Snead representing the USA.

• Above pictures
Hogan playing in the 1953 Open at Carnoustie, and with the Claret Jug after winning.

In 1955, Life magazine paid Hogan to reveal what he had learned. He confessed that he 'cupped' the left wrist just before reaching the top of the backswing. In 1957 he produced what is still one of the most influential instruction books ever published, Five Lessons: The Modern Fundamentals of Golf, written with Herbert Warren Wind. In it, Hogan further described the 'pronation' of the wrists on the backswing, something he said the old Scottish pros brought with them when they emigrated to America, as well as the importance of the left hip turning out of the way on the downswing to generate power. And he introduced a new image to the method-mad public: the pane of glass. He visualised a sheet of glass that ran from the ball up through the shoulders and indicated the proper plane of the swing. His ideas are still being debated, and tried, nearly 50 years later.

The Ladies' Game

Chapter SEVEN

When Mary Queen of Scots – one of the earliest known devotees of golf – said "keep your head down", you knew you'd better had, or else risk losing it! Whether she practised what she preached on the golf course, we'll never know. But she was certainly a keen golfer, known to have played a game only a few days after the murder of her husband. And her royal patronage would undoubtedly have helped spread the word about the game's attractions.

Ever since her day, women all over the world have embraced the game of golf. It wasn't until the mid-19th century, however, that the first ladies' golf clubs were formed. Around that time the women wore such restrictive clothing that it was impossible for them to exploit their sporting talents fully. It was even considered unladylike to swing the club above shoulder-height! In that kind of environment, the women's game was hardly likely to take off in a big way.

Things were soon to change, though. The Ladies' Golf Union was formed in 1893 and the women's game never looked back. By the early 1900s, women's golf was in good health on both sides of the Atlantic. As were the game's exponents, perhaps spurred by an article in The New York Times that began with the breathless assertion: "The woman who wants to be good and beautiful – which is to say healthy – must play golf...the best game ever introduced in America."

Healthy, then. But not very profitable. While the era of Ben Hogan, Byron Nelson, and Sam Snead transformed big-time golf into a game that was strictly for professionals, the top women players remained amateurs until after the Second World War. This is not to say that there weren't some very fine women golfers, though – including two that were downright magnificent.

During the 1920s, Joyce Wethered ruled Britannia, with a swing that was at once graceful and compact and an ever-buoyant temperament that served her well in match play. In one famous incident at Sheringham Golf Club, a fine links on the rugged north Norfolk coastline, she putted out while a steam train thundered past the green no more than 30 feet from where she was standing. After securing victory,

• Above
Mary Queen of Scots playing golf at St Andrews, 1563.

which was an almost inevitable outcome whenever the surname Wethered appeared on the draw sheet, she was asked by a journalist if the noise of the train hadn't put her off. Her reply was "what train?".

With focus like that, it was hardly surprising that Wethered seldom lost. She won four British Amateurs and five consecutive English Amateurs before retiring, as Bobby Jones did, at the tender age of 28. She, like Jones, obviously saw merit in the principle of quitting while you're ahead. And she was indeed ahead, streets ahead sometimes, of her rivals. It was Jones, in fact, who paid Wethered the ultimate compliment, calling her the finest golfer – man or woman – he had ever seen. "I have no hesitancy in saying," commented Jones "that accounting for the unavoidable handicap of a woman's lesser physical strength, she is the finest golfer I have ever seen." Praise does not come any higher than that.

Wethered's last British Amateur title, in 1929, was her most gratifying as it came at St Andrews with a narrow 2-up victory in the final match over the other powerhouse of women's golf, America's Glenna Collett.

No woman in the United States was a match for Glenna, who dominated the US Amateur with a record six victories, including three in a row from 1928–30, along with dozens of lesser events. Her single frustration was in never winning the British Amateur, but when Margaret and Harriott Curtis, a pair of former US Amateur Champions from Boston, donated a cup for international competition between America and Great Britain & Ireland, Glenna got a measure of satisfaction. The Curtis Cup was born – in essence, the women's amateur equivalent of the Ryder Cup – and Glenna was on the first six teams, captaining three of them. Over that stretch the US went undefeated.

Still, even after Wethered's winning era was past, the Women's British Amateur was dominated by

• Above
Joyce Wethered with the trophy after winning the 1929 Women's Open at St Andrews.

• Inset
Glenna Collett tastes victory from the Curtis Cup.

home players. It was 1947 before the title went to an American woman – the same woman who had won the 1946 US Amateur. She would completely change the face of women's golf around the world. Her name was Mildred, but everyone knew her as Babe.

Babe Didrikson was born in Texas – just like Ben Hogan and Byron Nelson – and just two years after them. But well before Ben and Byron made their marks, the Babe was famous worldwide.

Not, however, as a golfer. At the 1932 Olympic Games, she won two gold medals, in the javelin and 80-metre hurdles, and tied for first in the high jump before being disqualified on a technicality. She was a natural athlete, gifted at everything she tried – an All-American basketball player, accomplished swimmer and diver, expert rifle shot, bowler, figure skater, and bike racer, as well as a tennis player of tournament calibre. She even dabbled in baseball and football. No woman – and few men – could run, jump, throw, and hit like the Babe. She could win just about anything except the Kentucky Derby!

But golf – the last game she tried – became her one true love. And amazingly, she was even better at golf and it would soon completely outshine all her other significant sporting achievements combined.

The first formal round she played, she shot 93 while slugging out tee shots of 250 yards. In 1935, she won the first important tournament she entered, the Texas Women's Amateur Championship, holing a sand-wedge shot from a mud puddle for eagle to clinch the title.

But along with her native talent, Babe brought a work ethic that women's golf had never seen. She learned the game from Tommy Armour, who was not only a US and British Open Champion but also the finest teacher of his time. Babe worked diligently at what he taught her, playing and practising up to 16 hours a day. "I'd hit balls until my hands were bloody and sore," she said in her autobiography. "Then I'd hit some more with tape all over my hands and blood all over the tape."

Her first years were spent touring the country in exhibitions with the top men professionals, and later with her husband, professional wrestler George Zaharias. A born performer, the Babe lived for the limelight and entertained like a vaudevillian. When asked how a slender woman of 5 foot 7 could hit the ball so far she said, "I just hitch up my girdle and give it a rip."

Her exhibitions made her a professional in the

• Above
Babe Zaharias in action from 1946.

• Inset
The Babe was the most gifted female athlete the world had ever seen.

eyes of the USGA, but by 1944 she was reinstated as an amateur, and she wasted no time in making her mark, winning the 1946 US Women's Amateur and then the 1947 British Amateur at Gullane, Scotland, in a performance so overpowering that one of the local scribes said, "It seems cruel to send our girls out against a game like that."

The Babe then turned pro again, and made the astute decision to acquire the services of Fred Corcoran, a well-known sports agent who had handled the great Sam Snead and baseball slugger Ted Williams. Corcoran was a smart cookie and in the same year Babe signed with him, she signed a contract with Wilson Sporting Goods for $100,000. Corcoran and the Babe were probably the only twosome who could have pulled off a deal of that magnitude. The amount of money involved spoke volumes for their respective abilities.

So the Babe was making serious money – but what she really wanted was some serious competition, and an audience.

And so in 1950, to meet and exploit those needs, the Ladies Professional Golf Association was formed in the United States, with 11 women as its charter members and the Babe as its star attraction. Corcoran agreed to stage manage the tour, and Wilson paid the bills, but it was the women themselves who kept the books, wrote the cheques, handled the correspondence, and even called their own rulings.

Not surprisingly, the Babe dominated those early years. She won the money title four times in a row and along the way racked up an astonishing 31 tournament victories, including three Women's US Opens. And she likely would have won dozens more events, had her career not been curtailed by cancer.

She was diagnosed in 1953, and the doctor's prognosis was not good. "I don't know if surgery will cure her," he said, "but I will say that she never again will play golf of championship calibre."

But he didn't know the Babe. A mere fourteen weeks later she was back on the golf course, and the next year she won five tournaments including the US Open by a whopping 12 strokes. Three more victories came in 1955, but then the cancer returned. This battle proved too great even for a mighty character such as her. In 1956 Babe Zaharias died at the tragically young age of 42.

But Babe was not the only talent on that fledgling women's tour. Even on her best days she

• Above
Zaharias won 31 tournaments including three US Opens.

• Inset
The Babe and Patty Berg were two of the pioneers of the Ladies Professional Golf Association.

could be beaten by a freckle-faced tomboy named Patty Berg. She had come from the unlikely golf hotbed of Minnesota where speed skating and street football were part of her early training. But by the age of just 16 Patty had won the Minneapolis City Golf Championship and a year later she nearly won the US Amateur, losing in the final to Glenna Collett – now Mrs. Edwin Vare and then en route to her record sixth title. But Berg later went on to win the Amateur along with 28 other titles.

During the War she served in the women's Marines, then came out firing as a professional golfer with a victory in the first Women's US Open in 1946. Along with Babe Zaharias, Berg dominated women's pro golf for the next decade, amassing a career total of 44 wins.

Aside from her playing talents, Berg's most important legacy is as a tireless advocate for the game of golf. When the LPGA was formed, she was its first President, and her service to the game has never wavered. When she won the US Open she handed back the $500 cheque, asking officials to use the money to promote junior golf. It was a typically generous gesture. For more than half a century she has crossed America and circled the globe, giving instructional clinics and talking up the game to whoever would listen. Golf has never had a better ambassador than Patty Berg.

The two other top-notch players at the dawn of the LPGA were Louise Suggs and Betsy Rawls. Suggs had learned the game at age ten from her father, an Atlanta club pro, developing a swing with such blinding clubhead speed that people called her the female Ben Hogan. Before turning pro she won both the US and British Amateurs, then added two US Opens and an LPGA Championship, which rank among 50 career victories. A feisty competitor, she liked nothing more than to go head to head with

• Above pictures
Patty Berg in action in 1936. She won 55 tournaments around the world.

Patty and the Babe. "When we're going at it in a tournament," she said, "it's like three cats fighting over a plate of fish."

Just how good was Louise? When she won the 1949 US Women's Open, the Babe finished second...by 14 strokes. Enough said.

Rawls joined the tour in 1951 and won her first US Open the same year. She would add three more Open titles, two LPGA Championships, and 49 other events for a total of 55 victories that ranks third on the all-time list. Only one other player has won the Women's US Open four times – Mickey Wright.

Fittingly, when Wright played in her first Open, at age 19, it was 1954, the year of Babe Zaharias's final victory, and Mickey was paired with the Babe, whom she outdrove on several holes. She finished fourth that year, but in the decade that followed, Mickey Wright became the undisputed successor to the Babe while setting a new standard of excellence in women's professional golf.

In contrast to the effervescent Babe, Mickey was shy and retiring. But what she lacked in glamour she delivered in game, with a swing of surpassing grace and effortless power – a swing that to this day is called the finest golf has ever produced. Mickey joined the LPGA Tour in 1955, and from 1957 until 1965, there was no one who could touch her. Over that span she won 65 tournaments, nearly a third of those she entered. Her banner year was 1961 when she won ten events including the US Open, the LPGA Championship, and her own Mickey Wright Open in her home town of San Diego.

She followed with ten more wins in 1962, a record 13 in 1963 and 11 in 1964. Thereafter she went into semi-retirement, to rest an ailing wrist and pursue a college degree. Although Wright played sporadically during the next few years, and continued to win, she had made her decision. "All I ever wanted to be was the greatest woman golfer in the world," she said, "and I quit when I believed I had done that." Few could disagree with that blunt assertion.

The rise of Mickey Wright mirrored the steady growth of the LPGA, which in turn reflected the good times in America. After two decades of depression and war, the country had emerged into a period of expansion and prosperity – for more Americans than ever before, it was time to play golf. The same was true in Britain as well. New courses were popping up everywhere, and they weren't quite like the old ones. It had been a quarter-century since the heyday of architects Tillinghast, Ross, and Mackenzie, and in that time much had happened. Earth moving equipment had replaced horse-drawn scrapers, allowing designers to sculpt their visions from the dirt. Riding mowers had made courses easier and less expensive to maintain, while also producing mammoth greens and tees that gave the tractors room to turn around.

The prominent architects of the '20s and '30s had all passed away, but into the breach one man had stepped with confidence: Robert Trent Jones. Although a fine amateur player, Jones was no Bobby,

• Above
Mickey Wright set a new standard of excellence for women's golf.

• Above left
With 88 victories Kathy Whitworth is the most successful golfer of all time.

• Above right
In 1976 Judy Rankin became the first woman to surpass $100,000 in a single season.

so he turned his mind to design, becoming the first man to train specifically as a golf course architect. At Cornell University he devised his own curriculum, combining landscape design and agronomy. It was Rees Jones also who was called to Daytona, Florida, in 1993 to design the home course for the LPGA, a group of ladies who've come a long, long way.

With the retirement of Mickey Wright, a void had been left in women's golf. But, as one of her successors, Judy Rankin, rightly observed, "Mickey got the outside world to take a second look at women's golf, and when they looked, they discovered the rest of us."

The first one they noticed was a tall Texan named Kathy Whitworth, who led the LPGA money list in eight of the nine years between 1965 and 1973. No player in history – man or woman – has amassed more official victories than Whitworth who finished her career with 88 wins – four more than the leading man Sam Snead. In the process, she became the first woman golfer to surpass one million dollars in official prize winnings.

During that period, the women's game was totally dominated by Americans. Only Catherine Lacoste of France was able to loosen their grip on the game, sensationally winning the US Women's Open at the age of just 22. Not only that, she was still an amateur and at that time was the only overseas player to have taken the title.

In a similar milestone to Whitworth's, American Judy Rankin broke the $100,000 barrier for a single season when in 1976 she won seven events. However, Whitworth and Rankin, despite their spectacular achievements, went about their business in decidedly unspectacular fashion, and they were largely unappreciated.

But then there was JoAnne Carner, a long-hitting crowd-pleasing character in the tradition of Babe Zaharias. Her maiden name was Gunderson, and as an amateur she was known as The Great Gundy, winning every major title in sight, including the US Women's Amateur five times. She didn't turn pro until the age of 30, but once on Tour she lost little time in making her mark. In the decade and half starting in 1970, she won 42 LPGA titles and three million dollars in prize money, while adding a major dash of colour to women's golf.

In 1975, a young New York marketing mogul

named Ray Volpe took over as Commissioner of the LPGA. He stayed only seven years, but under his aggressive and imaginative leadership the tour's purses quadrupled while the televised events jumped from two to 14. During the same time, women's golf teams sprung up in colleges and universities across the country. The net effect of all this was that more and more talented women began joining the LPGA Tour.

One of them was named Nancy Lopez, and in this smiling young lady from Roswell, New Mexico, the LPGA found its first certified superstar. Like Arnold Palmer on the men's side, she arrived just in time for television, and oh did she put on a show. Lopez's swing may not have been classic, but it was devastatingly effective. Her rookie year was nothing short of phenomenal. She scored back-to-back victories before the season was two months old, and then, beginning in May, she won the next five events she entered – including the LPGA Championship – while capturing the attention and affection of sports fans everywhere. Before the year was out, Lopez had won nine times, established a new season scoring average, and earned more prize money than any rookie golfer, man or woman.

From there she just got better and better, winning 50 tournaments, along with legions of fans. Lopez remained the LPGA Tour's marquee attraction for 20 years. But at the same time, the supporting cast became stronger, deeper, and more compelling than ever as players such as Pat Bradley, Beth Daniel, Amy Alcott, Patty Sheehan and Betsy King took turns at the top and brought women's professional golf to a new level of prominence. "The best women golfers in the world" is the way the LPGA began billing itself, and today that is literally true, as Sweden's Annika Sorenstam, Australia's Karrie Webb and England's Laura Davies are the dominant players in a tour that has expanded its reach to include events in Canada, England, Australia, Japan and South Korea.

Beginning in the late 1990s and into the new millennium, the Far East proved itself to be a training

• ***Above left***
JoAnne Carner during the 1981 LPGA Championship.

• ***Above right***
Nancy Lopez from 1978, her rookie year, during which she won a record-breaking nine times.

ground for some of the world's most sensational young golfing talent, none more so than the extraordinary Se Ri Pak. Born in 1977, Pak didn't start playing golf until she was 14 years old. She was so gifted that she won 30 tournaments as an amateur and when she joined the professional ranks in 1996, won six of the 14 events she played in. She was on a roll and it didn't stop there.

When she joined the big time, the LPGA Tour, she was Rookie of the Year. But that was nothing. Along the way she'd won her first tournament, which also happened to be a major tournament, the LPGA Championship. Her second tour victory was also a major, the US Open. She then went and won the following week's tournament and two weeks later won again. And don't forget, this was all in her first year on tour. And she was just 22 years of age.

Pak was no flash in the pan, either. She'd won a couple more major championships before she'd turned 25 and soon proved herself to be the one person who could consistently get closest to undisputed World No.1 Annika Sorenstam.

Another golfer of Korean origin may have something to say about that, however. Michelle Wie, born and residing in Hawaii, shook up the golfing world when she tied for ninth place in the first major championship of 2003. Nothing remarkable about that – until you discover that Wie was 13 years old and had shot a third round 66 to put herself in contention for actually winning the tournament!

Already 6ft in height, with a statuesque and powerful golf swing, she's been tagged the Big Wiesy – a nod towards Ernie Els' nickname the 'Big Easy'. She and Ernie certainly share the same characteristics in their golf swing, using long levers to generate effortless power with elegance and style. And the two of them played together at the start of the 2004 season, when Wie received a special invitation to play in the Sony Open in Hawaii. After their practice round, Els said: "Michelle is very impressive; definitely the best swing of any woman golfer I've ever seen. For a young girl she's got all the shots; and she hits it a long way too."

In fact, nothing can prepare you for the shock of seeing for the first time Wei hit a golf ball. In Hawaii, her tee shots matched the average distance of the entire field. Despite a superb second round 68, Michelle was unlucky to miss the cut by a shot. But

• ***Above***
Se Ri Pak from Korea hits a shot during the final round of the 2002 McDonald's LPGA Championship, Delaware.

• ***Inset***
'Big Easy' with 'Big Wiesy' before the 2004 PGA Tour Sony Open.

she'd made an impression...big time! When she leaves school and turns professional, as she must surely go on to do, Wei may well inherit the golfing world.

As for women's golf in Europe, it experienced some difficult times in the 1980s and '90s, to the extent that many were writing the tour's obituary. But it proved itself to be resilient and at the start of the 21st century could look forward to building on foundations that were more secure than for many a year. Whether it can benefit in a meaningful way from the ripple effect of the burgeoning LPGA Tour in the States remains to be seen. Prize money on the Women's European Tour certainly has a long way to go to catch up with the big bucks on offer in the States.

Realistically it can at least hope to capitalise on the prestige of a few blue riband events in Europe, which attract strong fields, and also on the success of some of this continent's finest players, who also happen to be some of the best in the world.

The Women's British Open was the first, and one of the most deserving, beneficiaries. For years it struggled to assert itself on the world golf scene, until finally it was awarded major status to justify its famous title. With status came big prize money, the sort of loot a tournament must have in order to encourage already wealthy golfers to get on planes and want to be there on the first tee when the gun goes. The cache and the cash are an irresistible combination at The Women's British Open, assuring it a truly world class gathering of talent every year.

As does Solheim Cup week. Indeed, this event, launched in 1990, is one of the most significant, and welcome, developments in the women's game. This competition is essentially the women's equivalent of the Ryder Cup, contested biennially between the leading professionals in Europe and the United States. As such it has all the cut-and-thrust drama, excitement, and spectator appeal that we've come to associate with world class matchplay golf.

This tournament was named after Karsten Solheim, the brilliant founder of the famous Ping golf company. On paper, the idea showed great promise. In reality, it more than lived up to it. The only surprise, perhaps, is that no one thought of it earlier. But then again, 30 or 40 years ago it might have been a bit of a walkover for the mighty United States, so much so that the tournament may not have survived. As it was, Solheim's timing was inspired, for the launch of this contest coincided with a period when European golf was thriving as never before.

In Laura Davies Europe had one of the world's best golfers – and certainly the most exciting to

• Above left
Michelle Wie tees off on the 16th hole on her way to an impressive 68 during the second round of the 2004 Sony Open, Hawaii.

• Above right
Laura Davies celebrates after she birdies the second hole during the 1992 Solheim Cup at the Dalmahoy Golf Club in Scotland.

• Above
Davies kisses the Solheim Cup before the 1994 competition.

• Inset
Laura celebrates winning the 2004 AAMI Women's Australian Open. She has won at least one tournament every year since turning pro in 1985.

watch. Her hero was, and always has been, Seve Ballesteros. No coincidence then, that she played golf like him. Her technique may not have been perfect, but Davies possessed sublime talent.

She exploded on to the golfing scene in the mid-1980s, thumping drives in a fashion that set her apart from any other golfer of her generation. Her power hitting is rightly the stuff of legend. For anyone attending a women's tour event, there could surely be no greater shock, and treat, than watching Davies unleash a drive with seemingly no regard for the consequences. To go with the power, though, Davies had a strong all round game and a courageous, fighting spirit.

Having played in the 1984 Curtis Cup, Laura turned pro and promptly won her first tournament, the Belgian Open. She wasn't just the Rookie of the Year that season. She topped the money list, as well, as she did the following year. Soon, setting records came as naturally to Davies as her gift for hitting long drives. She holds the women's tour scoring record (20-under par), she's joint record-holder for the lowest score on tour (62), she holds the 54-hole scoring record (199), the biggest winning margin (16 strokes), and in 1994 was the first golfer, man or woman, to win on five different Tours in one calendar year. She has won more Solheim Cup points than any other golfer and in 1987 she was for a short while the holder of both the US and British Open titles. Oh, and she's won at least one tournament every year since turning professional in 1985, a remarkable achievement.

While Laura was still at her inspired best, along came the contrasting persona of Sweden's Annika Sorenstam. Her diminutive frame and unassuming manner fooled no one, for here was one of the greatest women's golf talents of all time. She is in some ways the Bjorn Borg of the women's golf scene – quiet, softly spoken, not one for outward shows of emotion, but a clinical, ruthless, winning machine.

When Sorenstam turned pro, there was no doubting her talent. She was leading individual in the 1992 World Amateur Team Championship and had blitzed the collegiate world while at the University of Arizona. But few could have predicted what she would soon go on to achieve.

She started off by winning the Rookie of the Year title in 1993 in Europe. She then went and claimed the same title in the United States in 1995, a year in which she became the first player in history to top both the European and LPGA Tour money lists in the same season. That year she also won her first US Open, which she retained in 1996 with a record score and an emphatic six stroke margin of victory. That was typical of Sorenstam. She is able to produce quite explosive streaks of low scoring, yet she does not in any way suffer the dips in form that so many golfers endure. Oh no. She is consistent. In fact, her game adheres to the principle that 'great golf isn't so much about the inspired shots you hit, as the bad shots you don't hit'. There isn't another golfer in the world, male or female, who makes fewer mistakes than Annika.

Sorenstam has the characteristics, both physical and mental, that mark her out as a champion. She has a good technique and swings the club with a beautiful, smooth rhythm. She hits almost every fairway she looks at, every green she aims at. And she putts like an angel. To cap it all, she has an unflappable, nerveless disposition and an ability to think clearly under pressure.

She has proved herself totally able to cope with any situation that the game can throw at her, confident in her abilities to get the job done. And why shouldn't she be. Let's make no bones about this, around the start of the 21st century she was the most dominant golfer in the world. Forget Tiger Woods. In the context of wins, top-three finishes, scoring averages relative to her nearest challengers – basically, any meaningful benchmark you'd care to mention – Annika was a class apart.

It has been suggested by many that her performance in 2002 is the greatest in the history of golf. Annika won an incredible 13 times around the world, and set or tied 20 LPGA records. From a total of 26 tournament starts, Annika won 13 events, and finished with 20 top 10s.

Together, Annika and Laura spearheaded Europe's challenge in the early years of the Solheim Cup, ably supported by a team of talented individuals driven by the collective passion and desire to win that characterises these team golf events.

The inaugural contest in 1990, played at Lake Nona in Florida, witnessed a powerful performance from the might of the United States team. But in the return match two years later at Dalmahoy in Scotland, Europe turned the tables in the most extraordinary fashion. Leading by a margin of just one point after

• Above
Annika Sorenstam, the undisputed queen of golf, on her way to winning the 1995 Women's US Open from the Broadmoor East Golf Course in Colorado Springs.

the first two days' foursomes and fourballs, the home side routed the supposedly stronger Americans in the singles matches by the comprehensive margin of 7-3. Leading the way, as always, was Laura Davies, beating the formidable Brandie Burton by 4&2. It was a stunning week's golf.

Karsten Solheim, who was there to present the cup to the winning team, could not have wished for a better start. And while his death robbed him of the pleasure of seeing many more of the contests that bore his name, he can surely rest easily in the knowledge that the Solheim Cup will prove to be as much a popular legacy to all golfers, whatever their gender, as the famous Ping clubs he created.

The Cup is in safe hands, then – as is the fate of women's golf. Like the men's professional game, women's golf has changed beyond all recognition in the last 100 years. But it's never looked in better health.

The Big Three

Chapter EIGHT

8

• **Above**
Jack Nicklaus, Gary Player and Arnold Palmer gather at the 2001 Senior British Open.

To most people the name of George S May does not mean a thing in the context of golf's Big Three – Arnold Palmer, Jack Nicklaus and Gary Player. But in actual fact, this flamboyant Chicago businessman played a pivotal role, by virtue of the fact that he launched the era of televised golf. May had an instinct for pleasing the public. He was the first to put up grandstands so more people could follow the action. He was the first to put up scoreboards to display up-to-the-minute scores of the leading players. And for a time he actually pinned numbers on the backs of the players so they could be more readily identified by the gallery.

But most of all, May was the first to put golf on TV – and what a moment he chose. In 1953, for the final round of his tournament, the World Championship of Golf, May positioned a single camera atop the grandstand at the 18th green of the Tam O'Shanter Country Club. Coming to that final hole, Lew Worsham needed a birdie three to reach a playoff for the $25,000 first prize – then the biggest pay-off in golf. After a perfect tee shot he faced a wedge approach of roughly 120 yards. His low, driving shot hit well short of the pin, but it rolled and rolled – nearly 60 feet – and dropped straight into the hole for an eagle two and outright victory.

With that magic moment – witnessed by a million incredulous viewers – everything changed, as television cast its electronic glow across the fairways of professional golf. In 1954, the US Open came to the tube, in 1955, the Masters, and by the early '60s every significant tournament was either on TV or trying to get there.

Arnold Palmer

With the stage set and the cameras in place, golf was ready for its first technicolor star, and he made his entrance in the form of Arnold Daniel Palmer. He was the classic American hero, with a swaggering gait, a ready smile, and the shoulders of an NFL fullback, straight out of the hills of Western Pennsylvania where his father, a steelworker turned golf professional, had been his only teacher, schooling him sternly in the fundamentals of good golf and good behaviour.

Arnold was three years old when he first picked up a club. At age seven he broke a hundred, at 14 he shot 71 in his first high school match, and by the time he entered Wake Forest University he had won

everything, with a go-for-broke style that sometimes put him in trouble and a hard-nosed resourcefulness that usually got him out. He didn't play a golf course, he beat it into submission, slashing and bashing and thrashing until it had no choice but to yield.

A victory in the 1954 US Amateur convinced him to turn pro, and he broke through four years later, winning the first of four Masters titles along with four other events. But it was in 1960 that Arnold Palmer truly began his reign. That April he arrived at Augusta with four wins already in his pocket, including three of them in succession. A first-round 67 gave him the Masters lead, and he held onto it until the final moments on Sunday when a fast-closing Ken Venturi pulled in front of him. Palmer came to the last two holes needing two birdies to win, and in spectacular style he got them both, holing a 35-footer at 17 and then knocking a 6-iron up the steep fairway to three feet from the flag at the final green. On that afternoon the Palmer Charge was born.

Six weeks later it became legendary. When Arnie went to the Cherry Hills Country Club in Denver, Colorado, he had one thing in mind: a US Open to go with his Masters. By the start of the final round, however, he was seven strokes off the lead, with 14 formidable players in front of him. In the clubhouse, shortly before heading out to play, he was approached by two friends from the press, Bob Drum and Dan Jenkins, who roasted him for his mediocre showing.

"There are some guys out there who think you're just an upstart, a flash in the pan," said Drum.

"What would happen if I shot 65 in the last round?" said Palmer testily.

"Nothing," said Drum, "you're out of it."

"It would give me a total of 280," said Palmer.

just about every school, county, and state-wide event worth winning.

The Palmer method was less than elegant – a wide stance, a quick wrench-away of the club, and then a lunge through impact to a club-flailing finish in which he looked as if he was snatching something back from a fire. But he pulverised the ball! His putting stroke was equally ungraceful, a hunch-shouldered, knock-kneed, pigeon-toed rap. But he rapped it home from everywhere.

Above all, however, what Arnold Palmer brought to the game was a bold and burning will to win. He had the perfect psyche for golf – a fighting spirit without a temper. Arnie gave it everything and tried

• Above
Arnold Palmer chips out of trouble at the 1967 World Matchplay at Wentworth.

• Above
Arnie with his caddie at Augusta. He won four US Masters in a glittering career.

• Opposite
Arnold Palmer struggles with his emotions as he waits to putt on the18th green during the second round of the 2004 Masters, his final appearance.

"That's the kind of number that wins the US Open."

"Yeah," laughed Jenkins, "when Hogan shoots it."

More determined than ever, Palmer climbed onto the tee of the par-4 first hole and did something he had tried boldly but unsuccessfully to do all week – he drove the green, 346 yards away. His two-putt birdie ignited the most explosive stretch of sub-par golf the Open had ever seen – four birdies in a row, six in the first seven holes – for a score of 30 on the outward nine.

Suddenly, Arnie was tied for the lead. Still in his path, however, was the best player of the era just past – Ben Hogan – playing side by side with the best player of the era to come – Jack Nicklaus. Hogan, at age 47, was making his last serious bid at an Open title while Nicklaus, age 20, was making his first.

But on that day in June of 1960, it was Arnie's turn. He closed with a seven-under-par 65 – precisely the score he had predicted – for a two-stroke victory. When, on the 18th green, he leaned back and hurled his visor to the sky, Arnold Palmer was the undisputed king of American golf.

He was a king with a common man's touch. When Arnie stood on a tee, he could make eye contact with every soul in the gallery – make each of them feel he was their best friend – and when he then hitched up his pants, they all knew the game was on. In contrast to his stolid predecessor Hogan, Arnie wore his emotions on his sleeve. When happy, he grinned; when unhappy, he grimaced – and his fans celebrated and suffered with him every step of the way.

They celebrated four Masters jackets and they suffered three playoff losses in the US Open. They celebrated back-to-back victories in the Open Championship, a championship whose prominence he single-handedly resurrected from its post-War doldrums, simply by playing in it each year. And they suffered as he struggled in vain to win the USPGA, the major title that eluded him just as tragically as

the US Open had eluded Sam Snead.

In all, Arnold Palmer won 60 US events, plus another 29 titles around the world. He led the money list four times, was the first player to win $100,000 in a single season and the first to reach a million dollars in career earnings. And with the help of his business manager, Mark McCormack, he built those earnings into an empire worth many millions more. But Arnold Palmer never lost his humility, or forgot the working-man's values his father had taught him. And while winning all those titles, and all that money, he also won the unmatched adoration of golf fans around the world. No player, before or since, has been loved so much by so many.

In a sense, Arnold Palmer sold golf to the American public, and his number-one customer was another national hero – Dwight Eisenhower – who picked up the game and brought it to the White House lawn. No one loved golf more than Ike, no one played it better than Arnie, and together they spread the gospel to millions of leisure-minded Americans.

Time hasn't withered his popularity, either. When Palmer was playing in his 50th and final Masters in 2004, he received the biggest ovation of the week – not just on the final fairway, but on every tee, fairway, green, and every step in between. He was genuinely moved, often to tears. So were many in the gallery. Even some of the top players hung out behind the 18th green to watch the great man finish. It was an emotional end of an era.

Between 1960 and 1970, golf in the United States boomed as never before. As the number of players doubled, from five million to ten, the number of courses exploded from 6,300 to 10,000 – in effect, a new golf course opened in America every day of the year for ten straight years.

But no aspect of the game grew more dramatically than the professional tour. For years it had been relatively stagnant. Except for the major championships and a couple of California pro-ams hosted by Bing Crosby and Bob Hope, the tour had been a succession of modest, community-run events with names like the Rubber City Open, the Nashville Invitational, and the Palm Beach Round Robin. But as the TV networks and commercial sponsors began to pay serious money for the right to beam Arnie & Co. into the homes of golf fans, pro golf became big business.

This growth did not come without pain. For a brief time a conflict brewed between the PGA of America, the tournament sponsors, and the players over who should receive the lion's share of the broadcast fees. The result was that the players split from their teaching-pro brethren in the PGA, taking most of the rights money with them. Joseph C. Dey, the highly respected executive director of the USGA, took over as the first Commissioner of the organisation that became known as the PGA Tour. In 1958, the total purse for the tour had been one million dollars. A decade later, when the PGA Tour was formed, the purses increased to five million. For the pros, the era of big-money had begun.

Jack Nicklaus

Not surprisingly, that era produced a legion of talented young players. But one fellow rose above them all – one fellow rose, indeed, above every professional ever to play the game: Jack Nicklaus. When he came to golf at the age of 10, the chunky kid from Columbus, Ohio, had a lot on his side. In Charlie Nicklaus, he had a devoted father who loved the game; in Scioto Country Club, he had a home course so formidable it had hosted a US Open won by Bobby Jones; and, in Scioto's club professional, Jack Grout, he had one of the finest instructors in the country, a mentor who would drum into him the importance of a rock-steady head, good balance, and a big, powerful swing.

But most of all, Jack Nicklaus had raw athletic talent. He shot 51 for the first nine holes he played. By the age of 13 he had broken 70 at Scioto, and at 16 he stunned a field full of club professionals and a handful of touring pros, winning the Ohio State Open title.

Jack's first step toward immortality came in the 1959 US Amateur Championship, played at the Broadmoor Resort in Colorado, where he scored a dramatic 18th-hole victory in the final match over the defending champion, Charlie Coe. Two years later he won both the Amateur and NCAA titles, and the year after that he joined the pro tour.

No player was more eagerly anticipated, and yet no player was more rudely greeted, by both the press and the public. They called him Fat Jack and Nick Louse, said he was too young, too heavy, too sombre, too slow – but the simple truth was, he wasn't Arnold

Palmer. The contrast between the two of them could not have been greater. Where Palmer warmed to the galleries, Nicklaus ignored them. As Arnie's face found a thousand expressions, Nicklaus maintained what one writer called a "state prison stare".

Their styles of play were equally divergent. While the dashing Palmer could turn an ordinary round into high drama, Jack had a knack for making even superb play look matter-of-fact. Granted, his drives were gargantuan, his irons majestic, and he putted with the touch of an angel, but he went about his business with the plodding monotony of a mailman.

The inevitable Palmer-Nicklaus showdown came halfway through Jack's rookie year, in the US Open at Oakmont. Despite his glittering amateur credentials, Jack had surprisingly not won in his first six months on the tour. He had scored a second-place finish, at Phoenix, but the winner that week had been Arnold Palmer...and his margin of victory was 13 strokes.

Oakmont – just a few miles from Pittsburgh – was smack in the heart of Palmer country, and Arnie's Army was never more staunchly behind their general, who treated them to four days of gallant golf. His 283 total put him in first place. But it also put him in a tie with young Nicklaus, who had wrapped himself in a week-long cocoon of concentration and played the best golf of his budding career.

In the playoff Jack gave the world its first look at a new standard of championship golf. Taking the lead at the first hole, he never let go. By the halfway mark he was ahead by three strokes, and that

• Opposite
Nicklaus in 1966 with the Open Golf Championship trophy, after winning by one stroke.

• Above pictures
Jack Nicklaus during his playoff victory over Doug Sanders in the 1970 Open Golf Championship, St Andrews, and with his wife holding the Claret Jug.

became his margin of victory. Thus, in his 17th tournament as a professional, Nicklaus won and won big – and the tremors were felt throughout the world of golf. A geological shift had taken place.

Jack won twice more before the end of that year. Then in 1963 he exploded for five wins, including both the Masters and the USPGA Championship. In a space of 18 months, the 23-year-old Nicklaus had become the man to beat, and he would remain exactly that for the next quarter century.

His idol was Bobby Jones, and like Jones, Jack geared his career around the major championships, carefully managing his practice and play in order to peak for the Masters, the US Open, the Open Championship, and the USPGA. When he won the 1966 Open Championship at Muirfield he became, at age 26, the youngest man to complete the career Grand Slam. And that was just the beginning.

Ultimately, Nicklaus would win a total of 18 major championships – six Masters, five USPGAs, four US Opens and three Open Championships – a record that no other player has remotely approached, or likely ever will. Although Tiger Woods would no doubt beg to differ, even his spectacular winning streak through the late 1990s and into the 2000s leaves him well short of Jack's Magic 18, still with a lot to do.

As Tiger does so often now, Nicklaus did not simply win, he won in convincing, commanding, occasionally superhuman style. His victory in the '65 Masters came by nine strokes with a then-record score of 271, a sustained display of dominance witnessed by Bobby Jones himself who pronounced it "the greatest performance in golf history" and then paid Jack the ultimate compliment: "He plays a game with which I'm not familiar." It took golf, or specifically Tiger Woods, more than 30 years to catch up and beat Nicklaus' scoring record at Augusta.

At one time or another Nicklaus held or shared the 18-hole and 72-hole scoring records for each of the four major championships. Five times he won two majors in the same year, and in 1972 he came within a whisker of duplicating Ben Hogan's Triple Crown, winning the Masters and US Open before

finishing second to Lee Trevino in the Open Championship.

Nicklaus didn't have it all his own way – at least, not always. Lee Trevino, with six major championships of his own, was one of a handful of world-class players who was able occasionally to put a dent in Jack's challenge. A truly world class ball striker and effervescent character, Trevino won only two Open Championships, but he won them back to back and they were momentous affairs. At Birkdale in 1971, he held his nerve supremely well on the back nine to take the title and edge out Nicklaus, as he had done a few months earlier in the US Open.

The next year at Muirfield, Trevino succeeded in stopping Nicklaus in his bear tracks, when he was charging full tilt towards his third straight major championship. Having won the Masters and the US Open earlier that year, the previously unthinkable achievement of a Grand Slam was in Nicklaus' sights. But Trevino thwarted him. Not only that, he well and truly knocked the stuffing out of Tony Jacklin with an outrageous chip shot that dived into the hole on the penultimate green and effectively won him the championship. Poor Jacklin was devastated and some say he was never again quite the same player after that bitter defeat.

• ***Opposite***
Nicklaus plays out of a bunker during the 1986 US Masters on his way to winning his 18th Major.

• ***Above***
Jack Nicklaus in action during the 1980 US Open on the Lower Course of the Baltusrol Golf Club in New Jersey.

• ***Inset***
Nicklaus wins the Claret Jug again in the 1978 Open at St Andrews.

• **Above left**
Gary Player in action at Royal Lytham, St Annes on his way to winning the 1974 Open.

• **Above right**
Player receives the coveted Green Jacket from Tom Watson in 1978.

Gary Player

A more enduring challenge came from the Man in Black, Gary Player, the emphatic little South African who in the 1960s had ranked alongside Nicklaus and Palmer as one of golf's big three.

Well before commercial air travel became commonplace, the peripatetic Player was buzzing around the globe. No athlete has logged more miles, and no golfer has won more events world-wide – 184 at the last count. Nine of those wins are major championships, and when he won the 1965 US Open at Hazeltine, Player joined Hogan and Sarazen in an elite club that would soon include Nicklaus, as the only players to complete a modern Grand Slam of victories in the four major championships. Only Tiger Woods has since joined them, to turn it into an ultra-exclusive, five-man club.

Gary Player was the template on which the modern golfer is now based. He was eating bananas on the golf course when virtually everyone else was taking a drag from a fag. Now every pro golfer watches what they eat. He was going to the gym and pumping weights, when everyone else thought he was mad. Now every pro goes to the gym. In many ways, he was ahead of his time.

And in character he had all the ingredients you could ever look for in a champion. He had a great temperament – gutsy, fiercely determined and able to get the job done when it really mattered. Sure, like any other golfer he had his share of disappointments, times when he seized defeat from the jaws of victory. But these painful episodes seemed to spur on Player, almost give him added determination to win when the opportunity arose.

Player won three Open Championships in three different decades, in itself a marvellous achievement. His first win at Muirfield in 1959 was a dominant performance, so much so he could afford the luxury, albeit unwanted, of taking a double-bogey six on the final hole. He still shot 68, though, and it was enough to give him a two-stroke margin of victory.

Perhaps the greatest of his Open wins involved a classic battle with Jack Nicklaus at Carnoustie in 1968. The fairway wood shot Player hit over the 'spectacle' bunkers on the fearsome par-5 14th to within two feet of the hole giving him the easiest of eagle-threes, was one of the best shots of his career,

and perhaps one of the most timely in championship history. It gave him a decisive lead, just as Nicklaus was starting to breathe down his neck and the talented Bob Charles and Billy Casper were in equally close attendance.

When he won his second USPGA title at Oakland Hills, he thumped his ball out of thick rough at a crucial stage of the tournament to within tapping-in distance. It was another stroke of genius from this man with the courageous heart and mind. What's more it was executed at exactly the right time, as was Player's gift, and to this day it is considered one of the greatest wedge shots of all time.

At times Player could charge just as well as the original charger himself, Arnold Palmer. This was never more evident than at the 1978 Masters, probably the most dramatic of Player's major victories. Aged 43 and supposedly past his best, Player didn't figure in anyone's list of potential winners – except, perhaps, his own. Trailing the leaders by some distance going into the final round, and to all intents and purposes out of the tournament, Player dug deep into his memory bank and birdied seven of his final ten holes for an astonishing eight-under par 64 that took the title by one stroke. After he'd holed the winning birdie putt on the final green, he got a bear hug from his playing partner – one Seve Ballesteros.

The fact is, the 1978 Masters pretty much summed up Player's attitude to golf. He never knew when he was beaten and never stopped trying. In his world, there was no such thing as a lost cause. Famously in his semi-final match against the gifted, smooth swinging Tony Lema in the 1965 World Matchplay Championship, a title he won on a record five occasions, he came back from a deficit of seven down at the halfway stage to tie the match after 36 holes and win on the first playoff hole. Player treated every shot like his life depended on it. And it paid off.

Player was incredibly dedicated, perhaps the hardest practiser of his time. Of course, he is originator of the now famous phrase, "the more I practise the luckier I get". Actually, he wasn't lucky at all. He had great skill and, while not possessing a flawless technique, he was immensely strong and made the best of what talent he had...and he had plenty. Even though he was out-hit by both his great rivals, Palmer and Nicklaus, Player was able to more than hold his own in such illustrious company. He was a fine mid-iron player and pitcher of the ball, an aggressive chipper and putter and probably the greatest bunker player the world has ever seen. Out of sand he would threaten the hole like most other golfers would from a mid- to long-range putt. Hardly surprising, then, that he was extraordinarily successful.

He sincerely believed in the principle that you need determination in order to succeed at anything, and that in the process you must also suffer. If suffering means hard work, Player suffered greatly.

• Above
Gary Player's 1974 Open victory was the eighth of his nine major wins.

As far as he was concerned, nothing in this life comes easy and he was prepared to work as hard as was required to achieve his goals. His work ethic has been extraordinary, his enthusiasm unquenchable and his desire to win overwhelming. Those statements are true even today.

Next on the scene to challenge the mighty Jack Nicklaus was a new generation. Johnny Miller, the golden-haired Californian who burst to prominence with a 63 in the final round of the 1973 US Open, went on to win two dozen events including the Open Championship at Birkdale in 1976 where he thwarted the challenge of not only Nicklaus but also the youthful Seve Ballesteros. But Miller suffered many times at the hands of Nicklaus, never more so than at the 1975 Masters, where Jack's outrageous, monstrously long birdie putt on the par-3 16th helped snatch victory from Miller and the unfortunate Tom Weiskopf.

Next to step up to the block was Kansas City's Tom Watson, who made the boldest mark of all, winning five Open Championships, including a thrilling tussle with Nicklaus at Turnberry in 1977, when the two of them lapped the rest of the field on Saturday and Sunday, Nicklaus shooting rounds of 66-66 to fall one short of Watson's 66-65. It is remembered by many as the greatest Open of all time and was capped with a stunning putt from Jack that travelled the entire width of the final green, dropping in for an improbable birdie three after he'd driven into the gorse bushes on the right side of the fairway. It was typical of Nicklaus that he could summon up one last, courageous effort. Fortunately for Watson, he had played a marvellous approach from the middle of the fairway and had only a three-footer to match Nicklaus' birdie and take the title. If that putt had been any longer, he might have become another of big Jack's victims.

As it was, it spurred Watson on to more daring deeds against the great man. Earlier that year he'd won his first Masters. In the 1981 Masters, he stared down Jack again and by the end of the day was slipping the Green Jacket on to his shoulders for the second time. Perhaps most memorably of all, at the 1982 US Open at Pebble Beach, Watson dramatically holed a seemingly impossible chip shot out of deep rough beside the 71st green, giving him the birdie he needed to secure victory.

Painful as it must have been, though, when Jack lost he lost graciously. And he always came back, marshalling his mind and muscles more effectively, and over a longer period, than any player with the exception of Sam Snead. Nicklaus was winning major championships before Player, Trevino, Miller, and Watson came along, and he was also winning them after they stopped. That is incredible.

In the process he also won over the fans – not with charisma and charm, as Arnie had, but with the enduring brilliance of his game. If you cared at all about golf, if you had any interest in what could be accomplished at the highest reaches of sport, then you had to root for Jack Nicklaus.

His last hurrah came in the 1986 Masters. By that time, he had transformed from the Golden Bear to the Olden Bear – from perennial favourite to sentimental favourite. He had not won a tournament in two years, not won a major in six. Most of the

• Above
Tom Watson holds aloft the Claret Jug after winning the epic 'Duel in the Sun' 1977 Open played at Turnberry.

• Opposite
Tom Watson lines up a putt on his way to victory in the 1982 Open from Royal Troon.

media, many of his fellow competitors, and even some of his most loyal fans agreed that Jack's championship days were over.

And with nine holes to go in that '86 Masters, they all seemed right. Nicklaus was five strokes off the lead, Seve Ballesteros was cruising along and looking for all the world like he was about to land his third Green Jacket. In order to win Nicklaus would not only have to play like blazes, he would have to beat some of the very best players from the generation that had succeeded his own.

And that is exactly what he did. With his son Jackie at his side, the 46-year-old Nicklaus reached into his past and summoned nine holes of the most electrifying golf the game has ever seen, blitzing through the back nine at Augusta in 30 strokes. For two glorious hours, the vintage Nicklaus returned. With a display of inspired shotmaking, brilliant putting, and plain old guts, Jack roared past his young rivals to a one-stroke victory and a record sixth green jacket. It is unlikely there will ever be another Masters to match it for drama and excitement.

Nicklaus' career is so incomparable, it's fruitless to mention his name in the same breath as any other player of the last 50 years. No one has won more Masters, no one has won more US Opens, no one has won more USPGAs, and although others have won more Open Championships, no one has finished second there as often as Nicklaus, who has an incredible seven runner-up finishes to go with his three victories. Indeed, along with his 18 championship titles Jack has finished second in the majors no fewer than 19 times.

Perhaps the best way to put that achievement into proper perspective is to ask which two players of the modern era – from the time of Hogan, Nelson, and Snead to today's modern stars – which two of them, when taken together, can claim 18 major professional wins and 19 runner-up finishes. The answer...is none.

If and when Tiger Woods manages to surpass Nicklaus' major record, and we can assume that even for him it is going to take some time yet, then we can perhaps start another debate. Until then, though, there is no point anyone wasting their breath. Nicklaus is still the greatest. And that, as they say, is that!

Famous Five

Chapter NINE

9

• Above
Nick Faldo of England, Sandy Lyle of Scotland, Ian Woosnam of Wales, Bernhard Langer of Germany and Seve Ballesteros of Spain pose after the 1992 US Masters in Augusta, Georgia, USA.

The year spanning April 1957 to March 1958 was a particularly good vintage for European golf. At least, that's one way to describe it. If we're being a bit more honest, we'd describe it as probably the most significant year in the history of golf on this side of the Atlantic. What happened, you might ask? Well, five bouncing babies came into this world. Their names were Seve Ballesteros (the eldest), Nick Faldo, Sandy Lyle, Bernhard Langer and Ian Woosnam (the youngest). Within a couple of decades, they would be responsible for transforming the face of European golf, putting it on the map in the most emphatic and glorious fashion.

Here's how this 'Famous Five' did it.

Seve Ballesteros

It is fitting that Seve should be the eldest of this group, albeit only by a few months, for it was he who led the European charge. He was born for a role such as this. It is impossible now to over-exaggerate Seve's impact on the game in the late 1970s. He exploded on to the scene in utterly sensational fashion. As if his raven-haired, latin good looks and film star smile were not enough to grab attention, he played golf like no one else, like his life depended on every swashbuckling swing of a club and every subtle stroke of the putter. It was as though a one man golfing circus had come to town. And everyone flocked to see him.

People forget how young Seve was when he started performing his own special brand of golfing miracle. At 19 he almost won the Open Championship at Birkdale in 1976, only just losing out to the hottest player in the world at that time, Johnny Miller. The precocious chip-and-run shot that he threaded through the greenside bunkers on the 72nd green, to save par and tie second with none other than Jack Nicklaus, was soon given the label "the shot that was heard around the world". At the very least, it was an emphatic statement of intent. Seve, little more than a schoolboy in age, was not running scared of the big boys. Far from it, he was chasing them! By the end of that year, still only 19 years of age, he had topped the European Money List, as he would the following two years before heading west to seek further fame and fortune in the United States.

By that time, he was Open Champion, after a trademark daredevil last round at Royal Lytham had snatched the trophy from under Hale Irwin's bespectacled nose. Irwin must have thought he needed his eyes testing again, because Seve smashed drives to every corner of the golf course, yet kept making pars and the occasional birdie.

• Above
Seve Ballesteros of Spain tees off on the 11th hole of the 2002 Telefonica Open de Madrid.

His powers of recovery always were extraordinary.

Amazingly, some American journalists at the time played down his escapades and even said that he'd never win the US Masters because his driving was too wild. Those who had played with him begged to differ. They knew from first-hand experience that the hacks had overlooked two things. First, Seve's driving wasn't nearly as wild as they thought; he was a smart thinker who knew what he was doing more than people credited. Second, and most crucially, the man was a genius. He won the Masters that year so easily it was like a stroll in the park.

Seve's game was made for Augusta. There was a bit more room off the tee than at most other championships, and no rough to speak of, so he could smash his driver as hard as he liked. And he liked to do that. At the time, he was one of the game's longest hitters. More significantly, Augusta's notoriously slick, sloping greens placed a huge emphasis on short game skills and in that department Seve was king. After all, as a young boy he'd taught himself to play golf with a 3-iron and some pebbles on the beach. With a sand-wedge and a balata ball, hey, chipping must have seemed like a piece of cake! He won his second green jacket in 1983, again at a canter, and everyone thought he'd go on to win at least a handful, perhaps more. But astonishingly, he never won the Masters again.

Indeed, from the age of 31 – theoretically a professional golfer's prime – Seve did not win another major. It's funny. Seve was the ultimate boy wonder, someone who achieved great things at a young age, yet in a sense you feel he under-achieved. Someone with that much talent at his fingertips should surely have got his hands on more major trophies. But no. He stuck on five, not shabby by any means. But not as many as he should have won. Nowhere near as many, in fact.

Perhaps the intensity of Seve's game meant it could burn brightly for only so long. Sadly, it turned out to be not nearly long enough. He was never the most consistent of golfers, even when he was in his prime, so when his game started to go off the boil while he was still only in his late thirties, everyone thought "oh, that's just the way Seve is, he'll soon be back". But he never has been back, not really. There was for a while the occasional glimpse of the old magic, but by the mid-1990s Seve had run out of tricks.

We've all got used to not seeing him on leaderboards, but that doesn't mean to say every golfer with a pulse doesn't miss him. The likes of Seve come around only once in a generation.

• Opposite
Seve in full cry during the 1988 Open at Royal Lytham St Annes.

• Above
Seve celebrates on the 18th fairway on his way to victory in the 1979 Open at Royal Lytham St Annes.

The Famous Five

Nick Faldo

Next into this world was Nick Faldo, on July 18 1957. Thirty years later, almost to the day, he stood triumphant in the mist at Muirfield, holding aloft the Claret Jug and celebrating his first major victory, the Open Championship. In fairly quick succession he would add a second and third Open title to his name, interspersed with three Masters wins. His tally of six major championships is tangible evidence of his right to be described as the greatest British golfer in history.

Faldo and golf didn't meet until soon after his 14th birthday, relatively late by the standards on which these things are judged, but he wasn't exactly what you'd call slow on the uptake. Within four years he was English Amateur champion, which is fast work however you look at it.

He turned pro a year later, and didn't waste much time in winning his first professional tournament, thereby catapulting himself into the 1977 Ryder Cup team. This was when the golfing world really started to sit up and take notice of Nick Faldo. Playing with Peter Oosterhuis in the first day fourballs and foursomes, he won both matches. Jack Nicklaus and Ray Floyd were among those early scalps. In the final day singles he came up against Tom Watson, the recently crowned Open Champion, and beat him too. Still only 20 years of age, Faldo was utterly at home in the company of the world's best golfers and didn't mind one little bit giving them a sound thrashing. It seemed outrageous at the time, but it soon became habit.

Faldo was the epitome of the complete golfing package. He was a long hitter, a fact almost forgotten these days, and his elegant upright swing produced towering iron shots. He had a sweet short game and, in common with all truly world class players, could putt the lights out when the mood took him. He became a lean, mean, winning machine and then...well, then he decided he needed a major overhaul. David Leadbetter, relatively unknown at the time, was to be the mechanic.

Much was made of Faldo's decision to remodel his swing. A tiny minority were wholly supportive, whereas there were many more who said he was madder than a box of frogs. Others were a little less melodramatic, but still voiced concerns. If it ain't broke, don't fix it, they said. We'll never know what Faldo would have done had he left well alone in the 1980s and kept on swinging his merry way. But what we do know is that after a couple of wilderness years, where he took time to get to grips with his new swing, he emerged better in every way, like the

• ***Opposite***
Nick Faldo in action during the final round of the 2003 Heineken Classic at Royal Melbourne Golf Club.

• ***Above***
Faldo putts to win the 1987 Open at Muirfield in Scotland.

six million dollar man, only worth more!

His ball-striking was elevated to the realms of near-perfection, almost Hogan-like in its quality and consistency. He even seemed mentally stronger, utterly bullet proof under pressure, but that can probably be attributed to the fact that his swing was more dependable. As he said after the Open Championship in 1983, "I've been close in a couple of Opens and not been able to finish the job. The problem is my technique – or lack of it." Now he had the body to go with the strong mind. For six or seven glorious years, Faldo was the dominant golfer in the world.

No one at that time pursued championships with quite the relish Faldo did. Certainly no one else prepared so fastidiously. And once on the golf course, he withdrew into a cocoon of concentration, applying total focus on the job at hand. This didn't endear him to everyone. Indeed, his single-minded approach and seeming lack of personality left him wide open to pot shots. He got stung a few times by the newspapers and for years endured a fractious relationship with the media. Faldo didn't laugh, didn't crack jokes, didn't talk to his playing partners. Big deal! When he was on the golf course, Faldo was interested in only one thing – making his clubs talk and the ball listen. "To pick a shot, go for it, and do it; that's the ultimate," he once said. He got closer to that goal than any other golfer of his generation.

Only in Britain could a sportsman be criticised for winning in the wrong way. As is so often the case when a sportsman suddenly isn't invincible – see how it happened with Steve Davis, Pete Sampras, et al – he starts to become more appreciated. In the late 1990s Faldo's golf was not a patch on what it had once been. The newspapers softened up on him and we saw the softer side of Faldo.

Still, as we move into the 21st century, who's to say Faldo is done with winning? He is the supreme competitor and is one of that rare breed who has been able to produce his best golf in the moments of most intense pressure. While physically he's not the golfer he once was, mentally the nuts and bolts are all intact. If his undying enthusiasm for the game, and sheer determination, got him into another winning position, you wouldn't put it past him to pull another major out of the bag. After all, Jack Nicklaus, whose performances on television first inspired Faldo to take up the game, won the Masters at 46. How fitting if Faldo were to do the same.

• Above left
David Leadbetter and Nick Faldo before the 1991 US Masters.

• Above right
Faldo kisses the trophy after winning the 1987 Open.

Bernhard Langer

The legendary teaching guru John Jacobs tells a great little story about Bernhard Langer, which in many ways sums up this remarkable man's career. Jacobs was in conversation with a German teaching professional in the early 1970s, who was telling him about a young assistant pro he had working for him at the time. "He is the most incredible ball-striker," enthused the teaching pro, "but he's an absolutely terrible putter." This teenager's name was Bernhard Langer.

How prophetic. Bernhard Langer has for the last 20 years been one of the best ball-strikers and shot-makers in Europe, but...and it's a big but, no one has suffered more agony on the greens. Since turning professional at an age when most youngsters are still doing exams in school, Langer has had to fight the worst affliction a golfer can get – the yips. It's a psychological condition, but the effects are tangibly physical. The muscles behave uncontrollably, as if with a will of their own, which can make holing even the shortest putts a total and utter nightmare. Imagine how that feels when you're a professional golfer, you're playing the game to earn a living – pressure enough in itself – and there are hundreds, thousands of people watching and thinking "how on earth did you miss that one?".

Traditionally, the yips hits golfers late in their careers, when the nerve-endings are a little raw after years of top-flight competition. At least that's what happened with the likes of, say, Ben Hogan and Sam Snead. The fact that Langer has had to deal with this pretty much from day one, and has since been phenomenally successful, tells you a lot about the quality of the rest of his game. It's exceptional, if you feel the need to ask.

Perhaps most amazing of all, though, is that Langer has for the most part been a very good putter indeed. He's won two Masters, after all, on the fastest and scariest greens in the world. Against all odds, the man has found a way to overcome his mental demons and somehow get the ball in the hole often enough to stay at the top in Europe for the best part of 20 years.

In order to perform that seemingly simple

• ***Above***
Bernhard Langer during the 1993 US Masters.

function he has had to resort to some highly unorthodox putting methods. At first, he sought solutions with a change of equipment, but soon that wasn't enough. So he switched from an orthodox putting stroke to a cross-handed grip, with the left hand below the right. That worked just fine – in fact, more than fine; he won the US Masters in 1985 holding off a spirited last day challenge from his great rival Seve Ballesteros.

But the cross-handed grip worked only for a while, before the yips came back to haunt him. So he found another method, where he clamped his left wrist against the shaft of the putter, clasping his forearm with his left hand. It looked utterly bizarre, although when the putts started dropping again Langer was surely having the last laugh. But again, the yips returned. So Langer went to the broomhandle putter and, for now, it's proving reliable. For how long, no one knows...probably not even Bernhard himself.

It almost goes without saying that Langer possesses special qualities. He has an inner strength – no doubt in some way thanks to his deeply held religious faith, but mainly one suspects gained through sheer hard work and determination. Given similar turmoil on the greens, most tour pros would have given up years ago and, sensing that banging your head against a brick wall might not be good for your sanity, settled for making a steadier if less spectacular living from teaching the game.

But Langer at no time thought of quitting. He just kept on playing.

Reading profiles and interviews with Langer, it can at times seem like his career is in some ways defined by his troubles with the "short stick", which does not do the man credit. The simple fact of the matter is, there are very few players in the history of golf in Europe who have been able to sustain the high quality of golf that Langer has for the last 25 or so years. And he's still competing, trying to add to his tally of more than 50 wins around the world, two Masters titles and career earnings in excess of an astonishing £9 million. These are genuinely outstanding numbers, whichever way you look at it. But if you factor in his troubles on the greens, it's a spectacular achievement.

This modest German from a poor background has elevated himself and his family to considerable and well deserved fortune, and no small amount of fame. One suspects he could do without either the fame or the fortune, for it is how he lives his life that is of greatest importance to Langer.

It should come as no surprise then, that he commands respect and genuine affection from inside and outside the fairway ropes. A man of integrity and manners, you just know he will be the model Ryder Cup captain in 2004, an honour he richly deserves. Great golfer. Thoroughly decent bloke.

• Opposite
Bernhard Langer plays a pitch shot on the second hole during the final round of the 2004 Masters. Langer defied his years to finish tied-4th.

• Above
Bernhard Langer of the European team misses that crucial putt on the 18th in the final singles match of the 1991 Ryder Cup as the USA win the trophy at Kiawah Island, USA.

• Inset
Langer congratulated by Seve having won the 1995 US Masters.

Sandy Lyle

Nick Faldo may have beaten Sandy Lyle into this world by the small margin of five months, but when it came to golf there was a time when it seemed like Lyle would pip Faldo to the post in almost everything they did. But then he did get a head start in taking up the game in the first place, knee high to a 9-iron when he first started taking swipes at little white balls. By the time he was 14, when Faldo was only just discovering golf, Lyle was reputedly hitting 600 balls a day. Bigger, stronger, and more talented than anyone else in his age group, it was though he could see his destiny clearly laid out ahead of him and that every ball struck would bring him one step nearer.

Whether Sandy had a sense of his own future or not, he certainly marched towards it like a man who knew where he was going. He was the archetypal boy wonder, playing for England boys at the age of 14, English Amateur champion at 17, and again at 19. He never once took a backward step, generating an effortless momentum which he carried into his pro career.

This is when Lyle and Faldo started to dovetail – at least in the professional sense, for they were never the best of friends; they were simply too different. Still, it gave the media two Brit stars to write about and the pair of them obliged by performing in a fashion that grabbed the sporting headlines for all the right reasons.

Sandy won the Open at Royal St George's in 1985, Nick won it at Muirfield two years later. Sandy won the US Masters in 1988, the first Brit in history to do so, Nick won it a year later. The pair of them were at the heart of Europe's Ryder Cup renaissance when, under the inspired leadership of Tony Jacklin,

they played like the genuine would-beaters they so evidently were.

During the mid-1980s Sandy seemed unstoppable. He had the golf game to win wherever in the world he chose to tee it up. In the driving department he was long, sensationally long in fact. In an era when when driver clubheads were made of timber, he could launch the ball distances that even in today's high-tech world would be considered long. And his prowess with a 1-iron is rightly legendary; he was quite simply the best in the world with that club and could propel it distances that other tour pros of the day might have thought a decent-length drive!

And allied to that great power, he always had such a soft touch both on and around the greens. He was the sort of player who was able to save shots to par where lesser players might have wasted one. And even if he did drop a shot or two here and there, he produced so many stunning strokes that he was always giving himself lots of birdie and eagle opportunities.

However, at the end of the 1980s and into the 1990s, the careers of Lyle and Faldo finally went their separate ways. No one could have predicted it, at

• Opposite
Sandy Lyle on his way to winning the 1998 US Masters.

• Above
Sandy Lyle hits a shot during the 2003 Buick Invitational at Torrey Pines Golf Course.

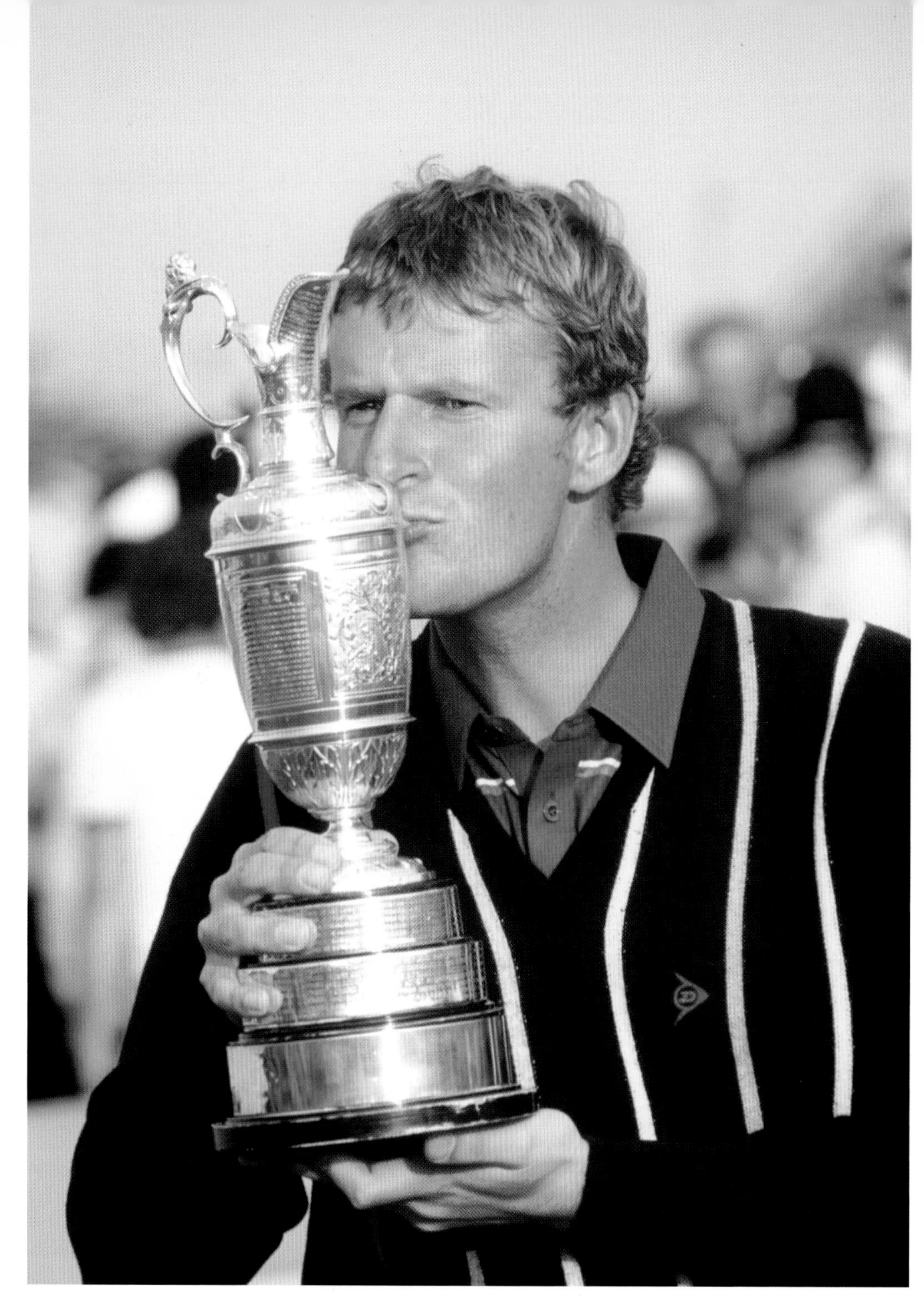

were nothing like each other personality-wise; Sandy is laid back and calm in his manner, whereas Seve is fiery and always demonstrative. But they both had an ability, if we can call it that, to hit the most appallingly wild shots, right smack bang in the middle of the most sublime golf. Even at his best, Sandy would hit drives that would finish in the next county – not that it fazed him in the least – and Seve was exactly the same. Maybe that's what warmed the Spaniard to the likeable Scot – he always was one of Sandy's biggest admirers and no doubt felt some affinity with the way he played. "When Sandy is good he is the best," said Seve on one occasion, "but when he is bad he is almost the worst." Sandy could be both in the same round of golf.

Maybe over the years the bad shots chipped away at his inner self-belief, maybe Sandy just forgot how to play well. Whatever, within three years of winning the Masters he was a shadow of his former self and he's since never even got close to recapturing his best form.

It seems harsh on such a nice man to dwell on his decline, though. Besides, he remains a wonderful golfer to watch. Even today there are few better sights on a practice range than Sandy swatting balls into the distance. It's majestic, just like it always was. The wins might have dried up, but Sandy is still the same unbelievably talented, amiable bloke with the laid-back nature, just like he always has been. It's nice to know that some things never change.

least not so soon. As Faldo went from strength to strength with his new-look swing, Sandy's game started to fall apart at the seams. He would be the first to admit that his swing, while immensely powerful and obviously effective, was never a thing of beauty. It seemed more reliant on instinct, feel, and sheer natural god-given talent.

In fact, although Faldo was Sandy's direct rival, due to their growing up together and competing on the boys' golf circuit, Sandy played the game more like his other great rival, Seve Ballesteros. The two

• Above
Lyle kisses the Claret Jug after winning the 1985 Open at Royal St George's Golf Club.

Ian Woosnam

In the context of Europe's so-called Famous Five, Ian Woosnam is the baby of the group. Not that this had anything to do with Woosie being the last among them to win his first European Tour event. The fact is, Woosie was more of a late developer. He turned pro around the same time as the rest of the Famous Five, but whereas they got straight on with the business of winning and amassing their first fortune, Woosie struggled, forced to travel around in a camper van eating baked beans out of a tin. It wasn't long before he had his own plane, though! With talent like Woosnam possesses, he was always destined to be a high flier.

Woosnam was born on the English side of the border, but to Welsh parents. He then learnt to play golf on a local course which had 15 holes in Wales, and only three in England, so it's fitting that as as golfing career blossomed he should fly the flag for Wales.

Although not tall, Woosnam soon developed a strong physique, which he credits with having worked on the family farm for six months soon after leaving school and spending his days lifting heavy hay bales. Having boxed as a small boy, he discovered that he could more than punch his weight on the golf course. He always was, and still is, a powerful ball-striker and an impressive one at that.

• Above
Ian Woosnam punches the air in triumph as he watches his winning putt on the 18th green during the 1991 US Masters at Augusta.

• Above left
Ian Woosnam sinks to his knees as his ball strikes the pin on the 17th green at the 1993 Ryder Cup, at The Belfry.

• Above right
Woosie celebrates victory after winning the 1987 World Matchplay Championship at Wentworth.

He's always had a much admired swing, too – admired not just by the huge galleries who have supported him over the years, drawn to his effortless and natural technique, but by his fellow professionals. Knowing what we know now, it seems amazing that it took so long for Woosnam to break through into the world of fat cheques and huge trophies. But that is indeed what happened. He had to go three times to the infamous European Tour Qualifying School, the graveyard of so many aspiring golf professionals, before he finally made enough cash on the main tour to retain his card. Once he had a foothold, though, Woosnam made great strides and fast.

He wasn't out of the top 11 on the money list for the next 12 years and in 1987, when he was riding high in the world rankings, won more than £1 million in prize money around the world. That year he was the first British player to win the World Matchplay, beating Sandy Lyle in a final that was memorable for the quality of its golf. Then in 2001 he became the first player ever to win the World Matchplay in three different decades and, aged 43, he was the oldest ever winner. That week he played golf of a standard to match anything in his 25-year pro career, simply emphasising his status as a player of true class.

So having been the last to make his mark on the professional circuit, Woosnam is now showing all the signs that he possesses the most enduring golf game among Europe's Famous Five. He is, and always has been, the epitome of a champion, his game blessed with all the ingredients of a real winner – tenacity, determination, bottle, a powerful long game and a delicate short game. His sheer passion for the game, and for competing, is evident in the way he strides

out purposefully between shots, with a bounce in his stride that suggests he can't wait to get to his ball and give it another whack. He really has been a great golfer to watch.

He would have surely won more than one major championship – the 1991 Masters – had it not been for his slight weakness with the putter. It has been a constant source of frustration to him, one which has never truly gone away. It's probably safe to say that there are few golfers in the world who have hit as many classy iron shots that subsequently didn't get converted with a holed putt. While he hasn't suffered quite as badly as, say, Bernhard Langer, it's been miserable enough to justify some praise in his ability to not get downcast or allow it to eat away at the rest of his game. Far from it. He's just kept peppering the pins.

And let's face it, he hasn't done too badly. Getting on for £8 million in career prize money and more than 40 tournament wins around the world. What he has won he's won in style, while all along he's been true to himself and lived exactly the way he wanted to live. He's hardly likely to have many regrets.

• Above
Woosie lifts the winning trophy after victory in the 2001 Cisco World Matchplay Championship.

• Inset
Lining up a putt during the 2004 British Masters at The Forest of Arden.

Ten Greatest Golf Courses

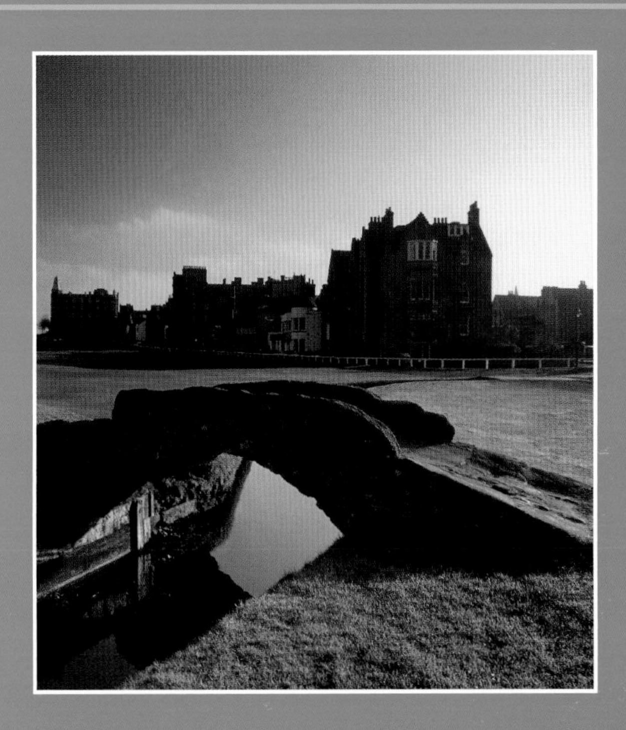

Chapter TEN

10

St Andrews

The Scots invented golf. Other nations have dug out ancient old drawings and dog-eared documents to try to add weight to their claim that they were the first to play the game, but it's no use. No one believes them, not really. The Scots did it and a great job they did, too. And this is where it all started, St Andrews.

This is the Home of Golf. Nowadays, there are more than 100 holes of golf on this hallowed turf on the east coast of Scotland. Despite the fact some of the newer layouts are very fine indeed, the main attraction, the Mecca, is the 'Old Course'. It's like nothing else on earth, which is hardly surprising since the only architects here were Mother Nature and generations of sheep. Pot bunkers, vast double greens, more humps and bumps than a teenager's duvet and wonderfully springy turf – it's an uplifting experience in more ways than one.

You stand on the first tee staring at the widest fairway in the game and, minutes later, you're

marching towards four hours of challenging, entertaining, joyous golf. You could argue that the best is saved for last...and second last. That'll be the 17th, arguably the most famous single golf hole in the world, bearing the innocent moniker 'Road Hole'. Making a double-bogey will never have seemed such fun! And the 18th, well, just savour the most famous view in golf as you aim your drive at the clock on the R&A clubhouse behind the green – and try to avoid hitting the old grey town on your right-hand side.

It may be a cliché in golf to highlight the merits of being able to follow in the footsteps of your heroes, something that only the privileged few are able to do in other sports, but when you come to St Andrews you truly understand the meaning of such things. Think of the great events you've seen here in the Open Championship – when you're playing the course, these memories cannot fail to touch you, they enhance the experience. Just think about who's played here – Bobby Jones, Jack Nicklaus, Arnold Palmer, Seve Ballesteros, Nick Faldo and Tiger Woods. And they all loved it. Given the choice of only one golf course to play for the rest of their lives, some of these illustrious names, not to mention thousands of others, would choose this above any other. It's awesome and unforgettable.

Every golfer should play here at least once and ideally many, many times. Because they say it gets better and better the more you play it.

• **Main**
View of the 1st hole on the Old Course at St Andrews in Fife, Scotland.

• **Inset**
General view of the Swilken Bridge and the Clubhouse on the Old Course at St Andrews.

Augusta National

Think of Augusta National and you immediately also think of the Masters. The two are inextricably linked, but unlike most other tournament/golf course relationships, in this case the golf course came first. Not that it was all that long ago. Only as recently as the 1930s did it become a glint in the eye of one man.

That man was Bobby Jones, a lawyer who in his spare time as an amateur golfer quite liked trawling handfuls of major championships. It was around this time that he'd decided that winning golf tournaments was all just a bit tedious. He needed a new challenge, something that would get his creative juices flowing. What better project than building one of the most beautiful golf courses in the world? That should do it. Jones wisely teamed up with Alister Mackenzie, the then doyen of golf course architecture, and together they created something truly special, unquestionably worthy of both their illustrious names.

Soon after the project was completed, Jones instigated a special invitational tournament. The Masters was born. For most of us, all that we know of this place is coloured with the vivid images of titanic struggles around the infamous loop of holes known as Amen Corner. It is no exaggeration to say that the 11th, 12th and 13th at Augusta are the most famous three holes in golf. They are also among the hardest, not least given the circumstances that golfers challenging for the coveted Green Jacket find themselves in.

The 11th features an unremarkable drive followed by an unnerving second shot, down hill to a kidney-

• Main
View of the 13th green at the US Masters at Augusta National in Georgia, USA.

• Inset
Looking towards the 12th green of the Augusta National.

shaped green guarded all too closely by water on the left side. The par-3 12th, played over water to a green only a dozen or so paces deep, is the closest a tour pro probably ever gets to a 'hit, hope and pray' shot – especially with the ever-present breeze swirling in a devious, unpredictable fashion. The same is true on the par-5 13th, as if it weren't hard enough. First you must manufacture your best slinging, 300-yard hook shot round the corner of this dogleg fairway. Then you're looking at a long-iron, off a sloping lie, to a green guarded by bunkers side and back, with Rae's Creek protecting the front. Sounds tough? It's tougher. Grown men have walked off this green utterly broken, dreams shattered.

The remaining 15 holes at Augusta may not have the strength in depth of other famous layouts, but what it can boast is perfection in grass. It is without a shadow of doubt the most perfectly manicured golf course in the world. The greens are like green velvet. And to walk those carpet-like fairways and take in the fresh Georgia air, perfumed with the aroma of a thousand azaleas and the like...could golf get any better? Probably not.

Shame it's harder to get a tee time here than it is a dinner date with Nicole Kidman. But where's the harm in dreaming?

Pebble Beach

They say in property that only three things really matter – location, location and location. Well, if the same principle were applied to the merits of golf courses, then Pebble Beach would be seriously desirable and just a bit on the expensive side. Perched on the west coast of the United States, on California's rugged Monterey Peninsula, this is a location to die for. It is a genuinely spectacular spot – not so much a stone's throw from the Pacific Ocean, more a gentle lob-wedge.

It's no coincidence that Pebble Beach has played host to some of the greatest US Opens in history. Jack Nicklaus in 1972, Tom Watson and his famous chip-in on the 17th in 1982, Tiger Woods and his astonishing 15-shot win in 2000. The truly great golf courses always bring out the best in the truly great players. It's what you might call a marriage made in golfing heaven.

You know something else that's great about Pebble Beach? Anyone can play here. Okay, so it's not cheap. But you can save up, pay your money and, just like at St Andrews, walk this hallowed turf and savour every step, every swing of the club, every holed putt.

Like so many championship courses, the essence of Pebble Beach is encapsulated in a few of its magnificent signature holes. The dinky little par-3 7th is the Jack Russell of the golfing world – small but, on the wrong kind of day, scary! Its yardage barely makes it into three figures, ordinarily sand wedge territory, but the line of play takes the golfer straight towards the Pacific Ocean. Not surprisingly, it can get a little breezy. And the green is narrow, very narrow. Bunkers and deep rough either side aren't what you'd call friendly. Quite frankly, even the pros get twitchy on this hole – but then, they're playing for high stakes. The rest of us can simply enjoy it for what it is – one of the best par-3s in the world.

The par-5 18th is one of the great holes in golf, period. The perfect drive flirts with the ocean front, as does the second shot as the fairway gently doglegs to the left. There was a time not so long ago when the 550-odd yardage kept the green out of reach in two, but nowadays tour pros are winging it on to the green with a drive and long-iron, such is the march of technology. In the real world, though, it's still a fearsome finishing hole.

Don't think Pebble is simply a two-hole wonder, though. The pros love it. And for thousands of amateur golfers who make long journeys from all over the world, Pebble Beach more than lives up to the hype.

• Opposite
View of Hole 18 at the Pebble Beach Golf Links in California.

• Inset
A golfer putting at the 7th green taken during the 1993 AT&T Pebble Beach National Pro-Am.

• Above
Picturesque view of the 13th.

Cypress Point

Next to one gorgeous house, there's usually another equally stunning pad. That's often true of golf courses, too. Certainly it's the case on California's Monterey Peninsula where, next door to Pebble Beach, lives Cypress Point. This is no poor relation, either. Okay, so most people prefer Pebble and in all the golf magazine rankings that count for anything it wins pretty much every time. But Cypress Point has its own charms and it's hard not to fall for them.

For starters, you've still got an eyeful of the same drop-dead gorgeous location. That counts for a lot. You've also got a fantastic golf course laid out before you, designed by the legend who was Dr Alister Mackenzie. If the great man were around today, he'd have to admit, probably in a modest way, that he had one of his good days when he put pen to paper on this plot of land. The fairways meander through avenues of huge Monterey cypress trees, leading to heavily contoured greens where generous smatterings of sculpted bunkers lie in wait.

If you're a big hitter, the front nine could easily be your happy hunting ground because it contains four par-5s; very unusual for a championship course, but great fun for the golfer. There's a couple of cracking par-3s in the mix, as well. It's not monstrously long, either, so early on you can really get a score going.

On the back nine there's no sign of a let-up in the entertainment stakes. Bravely, Mackenzie crafted the golf course with the emphasis firmly on shot-making, making sure he didn't succumb totally to the temptation to capitalise on the majestic views. Not that you'd notice. The par-3 16th is well over 200 yards, all of which requires an airborne carriage over the Pacific Ocean. Awesome, unforgiving, and definitely no free drops allowed. It's a similar scenario on the intimidating but spectacular 17th. Slice your drive here and you'll not just miss the fairway, but miss terra firma altogether. It's a shame for the resident fish population that golf balls aren't a particularly tasty morsel.

• ***Above***
View to the 15th hole at Cypress Point Country Club in Monterey, California.

• ***Opposite***
Cypress Point showing greens at the 15th, 16th & 17th.

• ***Opposite below***
A golfer tees off during the Bing Crosby Pro-Am at the treacherous par-3 16th.

It seems churlish to highlight weaknesses, but it must be said the 18th hole does not do justice to this wonderful layout. It's too short, only 340-odd yards, and doesn't exactly set the world alight for views, either. Ryder Cupper Jimmy Demaret, a superb American professional who won countless tournaments in the '40s and '50s, said Cypress was the "best 17-hole golf course in the world." It may at first seem a backhanded compliment, but perhaps it's not such a bad claim to fame. More tellingly, no one ever came away from Cypress anything other than invigorated by one of the most enthralling experiences the world of golf has to offer.

Royal County Down

When five-time Open champion and all-round golfing legend Tom Watson first played this course he said it included the finest consecutive 11 holes of links golf in the world. For the record, the other seven aren't shabby. Indeed Ronan Rafferty, the former European No1 who's probably played more golf courses than any other tour pro, says it is his favourite. Nothing on the planet beats it, he reckons. When the likes of Tom Watson and a golfing authority such as Ronan Rafferty say things like that, you just have to sit up and take notice.

Better still, don't just sit up. Grab your clubs, drive to the airport and book yourself a flight to Northern Ireland and a tee time on this epic golf course, preferably when the yellow gorse is in full bloom. You won't be disappointed. You'll probably want to stay. You'll certainly want to walk straight from the 18th green on to the first tee to do it all again. That's RCD for you.

If you don't fall in love with the front nine at Royal County Down, you surely aren't a golfer. It's as simple as that. In the mighty shadow of the purple and blue mountains of Mourne, the golf course follows the rugged curve of Dundrum Bay. You'll be captivated by the challenge that unfolds in front of you, revelling in an examination of golf that the famous writer Herbert Warren Wind described as the sternest of any he'd ever experienced. But – and here's a but you can only apply to Royal County Down – you'll almost get a stiff neck from looking back over your shoulder at the stunning views. It's a joyous dilemma not knowing which way to turn. Either way, you can't lose.

Happily, the short 4th hole changes the direction of play and turns you to face the mountains for the first time. From there on there's literally no respite for the golfing senses, as verdant green fairways weave through great, golden swathes of gorse either side. As we've said, it isn't easy. In fact, it can be uncompromisingly difficult. But this is one kind of punishment you could never get enough of.

Some say the blind tee shots – there are five in total – are a weak link in RCD's chain and that such trickery has no place on a championship golf course. There are even a couple of blind shots into greens. But these shots are only blind the first time you play them. And you'll surely be back again, so that takes care of that. There you go, then. RCD, the perfect golf course.

• Above
9th hole at the Royal County Down Golf Course, Northern Ireland.

• Inset
Royal County Down Clubhouse.

Royal Melbourne

If you're casting your eye across the golfing globe, in search of a place for the ideal golf holiday, you'll find plenty of places with greater concentrations of golf courses than Melbourne. But surely there are few cities which can boast such a cluster of top-quality layouts. The reason is the famous sand-belt area, which provides an embarrassment of riches for the travelling golfer. The best among them is the 36 holes to be found at Royal Melbourne which, when combined for championship tournaments, produce a composite course to rival the best in the world.

The landscape is not dissimilar to the natural terrain of a Scottish links, rugged and with an abundance of heather and bracken, so it is fitting that a Scotsman should have a hand in its creation. Enter Dr Alister Mackenzie, that man again, who teamed up with a former Australian Open champion Alex Russell. The success of their collective work can be best judged by the fact that it is undisputedly the best golf course in Australia and, some say, one of the best in the world.

In recent years the golf course has been blessed with the company of the world's finest golfers competing in the Heineken Classic. Ernie Els, who has won the title a few times, says it's one of his favourite courses. Not only that, he believes that Royal Melbourne has the best greens in the world. Els, like thousands of golfers before him, has found them a joy to putt on. There is literally not a putting surface in the world to compare with them.

Want to go there? Of course you do. But there are other reasons to make this pilgrimage to the south-west corner of Australia. Aside from the weather (although let's be honest, that's reason enough) it's a classic all-round test of golf. The bunkers aren't just for show, created in fancy shapes to look pretty. They're rugged in shape and represent genuine, avoid-at-all-costs hazards.

The undulations of the fairways and greens take perfect advantage of the natural rolling landscape. It's a real shot-makers golf course, which is why the likes of Ernie Els rate it so highly. The 18th is a stiff test even for today's super-talented tour pros armed with the latest weapons, a simply magnificent par-4 which is a worthy end game all of its own. Royal Melbourne rightly has a fearsome reputation as a stern test of golf. But that doesn't detract from the pleasure it brings to golfers of all standards. This is world-class golf for the masses. If only there were more like this.

• ***Above***
View of the 5th green at the Royal Melbourne course with its surrounding hazards.

• ***Inset***
View towards the 8th green.

Turnberry

At the time it might have seemed pathetically insignificant in the overall scheme of things, but the Ailsa course at Turnberry very nearly became a casualty of the Second World War. The old golf course had been dug up years earlier to build an airfield for the RAF. When the war was over, Turnberry very nearly remained buried under concrete. Happily it was rescued and given a new lease of life by the distinguished and talented architect Mackenzie Ross.

Turnberry was certainly worth saving. For one thing, it has a jaw-dropper of a location perched proudly on the west coast of Scotland, offering spectacular views across the Mull of Kintyre and over to the Isle of Arran. To the south-west, only the enchanting presence of Ailsa Craig, a giant

Christmas-pudding-shaped rock, interrupts the view out towards the horizon. Under a setting sun, there are few more captivating sights in the world of golf.

Amazingly, given the natural wonders of this place, it took a single weekend of championship golf to put Turnberry truly on the map. It was the 1977 Open Championship and Tom Watson and Jack Nicklaus, the two dominant golfers of the era, were locked in what many observers still believe was the greatest championship of all time. By the weekend their brilliance had long left the rest of the field trailing; they then battled head-to-head, punching and counter-punching with blows of inspiration and brilliance. Only a shot separated them at the end, Watson emerging victorious with a birdie of his own to match Nicklaus's outrageous long-range effort on the final green. The third-placed golfer was 12 shots adrift.

Thus Turnberry was blessed with a history to match the quality of the location. The golf course has gone from strength to strength ever since.

The three winners of the Open Championships held at Turnberry are Greg Norman, Tom Watson and Nick Price, all great drivers of the ball, which provides a clue as to the nature of the challenge. You don't necessarily have to be long, although that always helps, but you do have to be straight. This keeps you shy of the wiry grasses and dunes lining the fairways, and enables you to fire iron shots from the crisp, perfect turf and seek out the flags which are usually cunningly tucked away behind bunkers on the wonderfully contoured greens.

It is an awe-inspiring test of golf, cleverly crafted by Ross to capitalise fully on the magnificent location. As if it could not get any better, a short walk up the hill behind the 18th green brings you into the welcoming arms of the Turnberry Hotel – a place designed for sheer indulgence and luxury. Turnberry...what a place!

• Pictures
Sundown shots over Turnberry, clearly showing Ailsa Craig and the famous lighthouse.

Pine Valley

It must have taken great vision to conjure a great golf course out of 200 acres of unkempt forest and marshland in New Jersey. But then again, George Crump was that sort of man. A successful businessman and mad-keen golfer, he'd been looking for years for the perfect plot of land on which to fulfil his dream of building a golf course. He spotted this site while looking out of the window of a train he was travelling on. Great vision indeed.

Sadly, Crump wasn't around to see the completion of his dream. But no doubt he was looking down wearing a smile of satisfaction when Pine Valley finally opened just a year after his untimely death. Ever since then, Pine Valley has been for golfers what a honey pot is to bees. In other words, simply too good to resist.

This isn't your typical golf course. Because of the natural landscape, the fairways are laid out like green carpets between vast expanses of trees, undergrowth, water and sandy scrubland. You could not ask for better definition off the tee and nor could the consequences of missing a fairway be more apparent. It's a design feature that makes Pine Valley one of the world's great driving courses. Its fearsome reputation is well founded, as much for the psychological implications as anything else. You know all too well that if you hit it solidly off the tee, you can play from there. You may even stand a chance of playing to your handicap. However, if you miss too many fairways, it's goodnight.

• Main
The awesome 10th green.

• Inset
Looking along the 18th fairway at Pine Valley Golf Course.

The greens are designed and protected in similar fashion. Again, the landscape does its own very effective protection job. Cunning run-offs punish the slightly stray approach shots. Anything a little more wayward finds serious trouble. One of the greenside bunkers is called 'The Devil's Arse' which says it all really. Frankly, some of the traps are truly harrowing for those without an intimate knowledge of the workings of a sand wedge. But hey, playing out backwards is always an option.

In view of all this, then, it should perhaps come as no surprise to anyone that the Pine Valley members offer a standing bet to all first-time visitors, challenging them to break 80. The fact that this tradition has continued for so many years suggests not that the members are especially generous, more that they're a pretty shrewd bunch and know when they're on to a good thing.

While its reputation is rightly fearsome, Pine Valley remains at, or at least very near, the top of most golfers' wish lists.

Valderrama

When you're a billionaire, you can pretty much do what you like. We don't know this for sure, of course. But we can all imagine. Jaime Ortez Patino is a billionaire. When he decided he wanted to build the Augusta National of Europe, he didn't just imagine it. He did it. He got in touch with American golf course architect Robert Trent Jones and together they transformed an unremarkable layout in the south of Spain into Continental Europe's finest golf course.

Valderrama is a tribute to Patino's vision and commitment to doing something absolutely the best it can be done. No short cuts. No scrimping and saving. Just build the best golf course you can, money no object. He was rewarded with the Volvo Masters, the European Tour's season-ending grand

finale, and the ultimate prize in the form of the 1997 Ryder Cup matches. There Spain's greatest golfer, Seve Ballesteros, captained the European team to a memorable win over the might of the United States. Patino could not have asked for a better script to have been written.

One of the great things about Valderrama is that it's a fine championship test from the back tees, more than a challenge for Europe's best every year, and also a very playable golf course from the more forward tees, which means golfers of all standards can appreciate its charms...of which there are many.

Where to start? The greens, like Augusta's, are sublime. The grass is so fine that when closely mown, the putting surfaces are billiard-table smooth. The overall condition, again like the illustrious home of the Masters which so inspired Patino, is impeccable. The attention to detail is quite staggering and it makes the whole playing experience easy on the eye.

And technically speaking it's a fine layout. There is a good selection of holes which dogleg both ways, offering plenty of potential for the creative shot-makers to show off their skills. But the fairways aren't so narrow as to make the course unplayable to the average golfer. Instead, the main challenge lies in the second shots. Cork trees step out from the tree-lined fairways, tiptoeing on to the fairway and partially blocking the line to the flag from certain points. Hence to get at the pins and set up birdie putts, you need to place your ball in the correct portion of the fairway. Extensive greenside bunkering, with almost bright white sand, represents an aesthetically pleasing, but functional, form of added protection. All of this ensures that a good score is not easily teased out of Valderrama's grip.

Whatever the numbers at the bottom of the scorecard, a round of golf at Valderrama is something to savour, without doubt an experience you'll want to repeat at the earliest opportunity.

• ***Main***
View of Valderrama's 14th hole.

• ***Inset***
The first round of the 2002 Volvo Masters at Valderrama.

Muirfield

It is fair to say that one of the more accurate barometers of a golf course's credentials is its roll call of championship winners. Let us for a moment, then, dwell on the names of the golfers who have won an Open Championship at Muirfield. Introducing Walter Hagen, Henry Cotton, Gary Player, Jack Nicklaus, Lee Trevino, Tom Watson and Nick Faldo...honestly, what more do you need to know? A bit more? Okay, here goes then.

Muirfield is basically one of the purest, fairest, stiffest, classic tests of links golf that exists in the world today. Some say it is the finest of them all. It engages the golfer in a way that some modern-day designs simply cannot match. Old Tom Morris, the great grandfather of golf, who originally penned the layout for this course, and Harry Colt, who in the 1920s tweaked it into its current form, produced a masterpiece. Nick Faldo for one says it's his favourite. Jack Nicklaus loves it so much that he named one of his own golf courses Muirfield Village.

So what is it about this course that attracts such praise? Well, it could easily be summed up in one telling phrase: "What you see is what you get." Muirfield is not tricked up in any way. When you stand on the tee, everything is there in front of you. The ideal line, the potential hazards, basically all the visual information you need to pick the right shot and avoid hitting the wrong one. When you're on the fairway, staring at the green in the distance, it's the same story. You can see the dangers just as clearly as you can see the targets.

If that sounds like it might be a tad on the predictable side, a bit one-dimensional perhaps, you would be wrong. Very wrong. Muirfield is a shot-

• Main
View of the par-3 16th hole at the Muirfield Golf and Country Club in Edinburgh, Scotland.

• Inset
The par-3 13th hole.

maker's heaven on earth. The humps, hollows and gentle undulations of the fairways and greens are seemingly made for golf. In among all this are 160 or so bunkers, an unusually high number by any standards, but you can see where they are so golfers can have no complaints if they stumble upon them.

You could say that this is a consistent theme at Muirfield. Good shots get rewarded. Bad shots get punished, although, like all links golf courses, the capriciousness of the bounce can produce good or bad breaks, depending on whether it's your lucky day or not. But what are we saying? This is Muirfield. If you're playing here, it's definitely, 100 per cent, your lucky day.

21st Century Golf

Chapter ELEVEN

11

• Above
Tiger Woods and Ernie Els walk off the 16th hole during the third round of the 2003 Bay Hill Invitational in Florida.

100 years doesn't seem that long, does it? But when you see that the game of golf in this period is bookended by the contrasting images of Harry Vardon – he of the tweed jacket, tie and dodgy flat cap – and Tiger Woods...well, it suddenly seems like an awfully long time. And barely even the same game.

It's a shame the likes of Vardon, James Braid, and JH Taylor – golf's first Great Triumvirate who dominated golf around the start of the 20th century – couldn't pop down for a quick game today. What on earth would they make of it? For a proper welcome, befitting of such a classy threeball, we'd put them on, say, Augusta National. That would open their eyes a bit. And maybe we could persuade Tiger Woods to make up a fourball and have him tee off first, so he can rocket launch one of his drives 340 yards through the air. Can you imagine their faces?

We'd have to kit out the three old timers in appropriate garb, as well. Make them wear long trousers, for a start. None of those silly plus-fours. Give them a soft cotton shirt instead of a starchy collar and tie. Then the real fun begins. We'd swap their hickory-shafts for graphite, their crude clubheads for high-tech perimeter-weighted models with super-grippy grooves, their wooden-headed drivers for space-age titanium, and their primitive golf balls for high-spinning, long-distance, rubber bullets. By then they'd scarcely recognise it as even the same game, although it's fairly safe to assume they would enjoy the extra 100-yard walk from the tee to their golf ball. That would put a spring in their steps.

Mind you, 7,000-yard golf courses are not what they're used to. More like 6,000 in their day. Still, we could always arrange for an electric trolley...no, on second thoughts, forget that idea. You can't beat a good old-fashioned caddie. At least that hasn't changed.

Anyway, enough fantasy. What this scenario does is pose a serious question. Is golf going to change as much in the next 100 years as it did in the last 100? It seems incomprehensible. But as the 21st century gets properly into its stride, the game is moving at a rate that suggests almost anything is possible. Perhaps the more pressing question then is this; do we want it to change as much?

Let's face it, golf's doing just fine at the moment. Look at the top players. We are in the middle of the

era of the Tiger, who may in the next decade or so compile a record to support his already strong claim to be the greatest golfer who ever lived, and we can count ourselves genuinely fortunate to be so. Like those who saw Muhammad Ali box, or Pele play football, we should savour the moments when we see Tiger in full flow. When he creates history with another astonishing, record-breaking performance, no one should dare say "it's boring, it's bad for golf" or "it's predictable". Really, what we should be saying is "I'm glad I was around to see this" because it is not unreasonable to assume that there may not be another golfer as good as him in our lifetime, maybe not ever! That is not as fanciful or as sensationalist as it might sound.

But planet golf does not revolve solely around Tiger Woods. We have Ernie Els. We're not looking so much at a Great Triumvirate then, more of an Awesome Twosome. Before Tiger came along, South African Ernie Els was touted as the man most likely to dominate the world golf scene. And for a while he lived up to that promise. He won a hat-trick of South African titles – the Masters, PGA and Open – in one season, an achievement that prompted Gary Player

• ***Above***
Tiger shakes Ernie's hand after holing a 15-foot putt to win their playoff for the 1998 Johnnie Walker Classic played at Blue Canyon, Thailand.

• ***Below***
Tiger and Ernie look over a green during the final round of the 2002 NEC Invitational at Sahalee Country Club.

to say, "When I first saw Ernie play golf I knew I was witnessing one of golf's next generation of superstars." Seve Ballesteros, said he was "a golfer from another planet". He certainly gave that impression.

Soon after joining the European Tour, he travelled to Dubai for the Desert Classic and tore the Emirates golf course apart, shooting a first round 61, 11-under par, that had everyone scratching their heads in bewilderment. Ten years later, it is still regarded as one of the all-time great rounds in the history of the European Tour – even though it took place in the desert, and not in Europe, but hey, stretching golf's geographical boundaries is one aspect of the game's development that should be applauded and encouraged, not derided.

Ernie certainly fully embraced that principle and soon embarked on a kind of global smash and grab of golf's trophy cabinet. In 1994, he won his first US Open at Oakmont, a brutal layout which he conquered with a display of mature golf, powerful hitting and remarkably assured holing-out. He was aged only 24, and it was the sort of performance that marked him out as something truly special. That year he won three separate world titles, to further emphasise his newly acquired status as a global force. It sat comfortably on his broad shoulders.

In 1997 he won his second US Open at Congressional Country Club, another uncompromising layout set-up as only the USGA know how – punishing rough, narrow fairways and firm greens. Over the years Els has shown himself to be very much at home on the world's toughest golf courses and again, this was a typically complete performance from the big man. He stayed calm, played composed golf, and when the moment of truth arrived, he stepped up and produced a decisive shot of devastating brilliance to close the door on his closest challengers, one of whom happened to be his playing partner Colin Montgomerie.

The hole in question was the par-4 17th, a difficult hole with water guarding the left portion of the green. With the pin tucked away on the left corner, perilously close to the water, Ernie struck a nerveless 5-iron, which honed in on the elusive pin position. It was the shot of the tournament and, almost unanimously in the mind of anyone whose opinion counted for something, the shot of the year.

Ernie had to endure a few near misses in the

• Above left
Ernie Els with his wife Liesl and the trophy after winning the 1997 US Open at the Congressional Country Club.

• Above right
Ernie lifts the trophy after victory in the 1994 US Open at Oakmont Country Club.

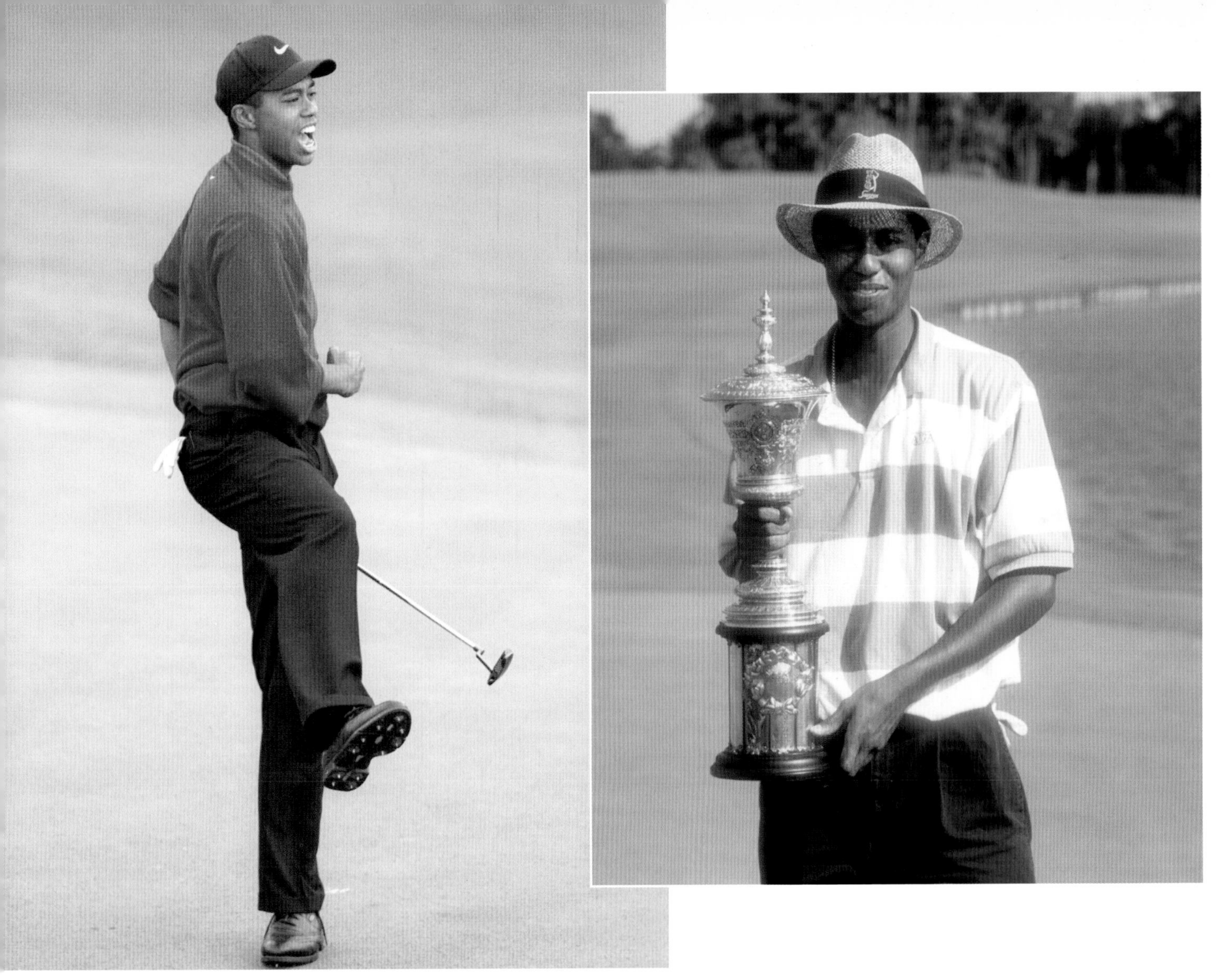

middle of those two US Open wins, but he was gathering mainstream trophies faster than any other golfer and it was seemingly just a matter of time before he added a handful of other majors to his collection. Indeed, he looked like the only man in the world capable of winning all four, joining Jack Nicklaus, Ben Hogan, Gene Sarazen and Gary Player in golf's most exclusive major club.

Then for no reason that anyone can fathom, Ernie went off the boil. By other golfer's standards, he wasn't doing too badly. He continued to win tournaments all over the world – although not with quite such regularity as before – and he was frequently a factor in major championships. But he wasn't winning major championships. And when you're as talented as Ernie Els, that's how you're judged – fairly or not.

To make matters worse, from Ernie's perspective at least, Tiger had since come along and taken over as the best player on the planet. This was not what you'd call the biggest surprise in the world. Far from it. Everyone saw him coming, at first admittedly as just a dot on the radar, but closing in fast. If we are to believe his dad, Tiger switched to an interlocking grip when he was in nappies and, as he first stumbled out of his pram, took a swipe at his dummy and sent it flying through an open window...with a touch of draw.

Only kidding. What did happen, though, was he won three straight US Junior Amateur Championships, then three straight US Amateur Championships. Not even the great Bobby Jones could hold a candle to that kind of amateur record. When he turned pro, things got just plain silly.

In his first major championship as a professional, the 1997 US Masters, records fell like ninepins. Having played the front nine in a disappointing, and at times sloppy, 40 strokes, he engineered a

• Above left
Tiger Woods celebrates after making a par putt to win the 1997 US Masters.

• Above right
Tiger with the trophy having won the 1994 US Amateur title in Ponte Vedra Beach, Florida.

genuinely incredible turnaround. He blitzed the back nine in 30 to finish with a two-under-par 70, then gathered momentum shooting 66, 65 on Friday and Saturday. Then on Sunday – when his nearest challengers were so far behind they needed binoculars to see him – he cruised to a closing 69.

By the end of the week, Tiger was wearing a green jacket and the record books looked like this. He'd beaten Jack Nicklaus' lowest ever 72-hole total (270), set the largest 54-hole lead (nine shots), the largest winning margin (12 shots), the most shots under par for the back nine (-16), the most threes in one week (26)...oh, and he was the youngest ever winner (21 years, 3 months and 14 days). Incredible.

He's since done much the same in other major championships as well. More remarkable even than that performance at Augusta, Tiger won the centenary US Open at Pebble Beach in 2000 by 15 shots. Yes, 15 shots! In a week where no other golfer managed to finish under par, Tiger was 12-under par. It was one of the biggest walkovers in the history of sport, let alone golf. It was further evidence, not that anyone needed reminding, that when Tiger gets into his stride, he is like a runaway train – frighteningly unstoppable.

That same year he won the Open Championship at the Home of Golf by a similarly impressive eight shots, thereby becoming only the fifth man in history to win all four of golf's major championships. It was fitting that he should select this celebrated venue to achieve such a significant feat – and his winner's speech was a mature performance which clearly showed Tiger's respect for the history of the game and its traditions.

But even that Open win paled into insignificance when soon afterwards he was in possession of all four major trophies at the same time. Technically, it wasn't a Grand Slam. Not in the true meaning of the word, anyway. It wasn't in the same calendar year. But in every other respect it was a Grand Slam and, as achievements go, it was nothing short of spectacular.

We could go on and on. And Tiger will. But in 2003 and into 2004 he has at least proved that he is human, after all. Tiger hasn't been in what you'd call a slump. The man has continued to win tournaments on the PGA Tour. But he hasn't won majors. Indeed, he's played quite poorly in majors; in the late 1990s that was almost unthinkable. Even the great Nicklaus had periods in his career where majors were hard to come by, but it didn't mean he was all washed up. Nor does Tiger's lean spell signal the end of his major-winning days.

Ever since he was a young kid, Tiger has admired Nicklaus and even had a chart on his bedroom wall tracking Jack's performances after turning professional. The symmetry between these two

• Above
Tiger beautifully silhouetted against the stunning Pebble Beach course in 2000.

• Inset
Tiger Woods holds the Claret Jug after his victory in the 2000 Open Championship at the Old Course, St Andrews.

golfers' careers is not just an indication of Tiger's talent, for no one else has managed to achieve as much at such a young age, but also an omen of what we can expect in the future. Tiger's got his eyes on Jack's record of 18 professional major victories. For him to surpass that landmark is a tall order, although it will be fun to watch him try.

But as he marches relentlessly towards that goal as he surely will, he is predicted to become golf's first ever billionaire. Unless a strange mood comes over him and he grows bored of winning, or injury cruelly cuts short his career, that extraordinary fiscal landmark is surely a foregone conclusion. Winning is his only motivation. Money has long ceased to be of any relevance.

Can anyone stop him? Well, stop him in his tracks? No. But check his stride from time to time, trip him up, and win more than just the occasional major championship? Maybe Ernie Els is the man who can.

Just when everyone thought the big man was going to cruise through his golfing life with an easy swagger, Ernie managed to put on a bit of a sprint. More than any other golfer he responded to the challenge set by Tiger at the beginning of the 21st century. He completely reassessed every single aspect of his life – his fitness, his golf swing, his short game, his mind, even the way he organised his family life – in order to achieve one single, crystal-clear objective; to become the best player in the world again.

The subsequent results were a cast-iron endorsement of the man's talent and the seriousness of his intentions. In short time he added an Open Championship to his two US Opens, lifting the claret jug at one of his favourite courses, Muirfield. That week all the best things about Ernie's game were in evidence. His second round 66 was sublime, a display of effortless power and precision play. His

• ***Above left***
Ernie Els in action on the ninth fairway on his way to winning the 2002 Open at Muirfield.

• ***Above right***
Ernie urges his ball to the pin on the way to a course record 12-under-par 60 during the first round of the Heineken Classic at the Royal Melbourne golf course.

• **Above**
Phil Mickelson leaps in the air after sinking his birdie putt to win the 2004 Masters by one shot from Ernie Els.

final round stumble on the par-3 16th – when the title appeared to be in the bag – revealed the fallible, human side that makes the man so popular. And the way he pulled himself together, birdieing the very next hole and emerging triumphant from the subsequent four-man playoff, was a tribute to his courageous heart and strong mind.

The 2002 Open was just the platform Els needed to relaunch his career. At Wentworth later that year he played one of the most astonishing rounds in the history of the World Matchplay Championship, a 12-under-par 60 that lit up the West Course on a gloomy autumnal day. Colin Montgomerie was again on the receiving end of this Ernie barrage of brilliance.

From that moment on, Ernie had the impetus to propel his huge frame and awesome golf game to new heights. At the start of 2003 he stunned the rest of the field who had come to Hawaii for the USPGA Tour's curtain-raiser, the Mercedes Championship, averaging 65 over the four rounds. His 31-under par aggregate smashed the existing US Tour scoring record and set a new benchmark for the world's best to shoot at in years to come.

By the end of February, he'd won four of the six tournaments he'd entered. By the end of the year, he'd won seven times and bagged the top spot on Europe's Order of Merit. He started the 2004 season in similar fashion, winning twice in quick succession on the PGA and European Tours. It included surely the round of the year, a 12-under-par 60 at Royal Melbourne, a score that many thought impossible on a course of such pedigree. But Ernie can do that kind of thing; make the extraordinary look rather easy. Suddenly, Ernie looks like a man who could maybe win the complete set of majors. Whether he topples the mighty Tiger is almost irrelevant. Of more importance is the promise of the two of them challenging one another as they play their best golf for many years to come. For all the world they look set to provide golf fans with a feast of competitive entertainment. Looking back over the last century, every segment of time has been defined by a rivalry between two or three standout players. The beginning of the 21st century will possibly be remembered as the Tiger and Ernie years.

But these two might not have it all their own way. Indeed, golf at the highest level could not be found wanting of a more serious collective challenge than is apparent now. Phil Mickelson and Vijay Singh are two players in particular who have raised their games to new heights.

Vijay is a class act, a hard worker with a sublime and almost effortless golf swing. He's a model of consistency, too, able to register wins and top-10 finishes with a regularity that makes a mockery of the strength in depth that exists on the PGA Tour. And Phil, of course, is finally a major-winner having taken the 2004 Masters in spectacular fashion. It was by common consensus the most exciting Masters since Jack Nicklaus took the title way back in 1986. Phil's incredible back-nine performance on that memorable Sunday, where he pipped Ernie Els with a stunning last-hole birdie-three, must surely give him the confidence he needs to challenge again for golf's top honours.

Then there's the new breed of young guns. The way the game is taught in the 21st century means that young golfers have access to standards of tuition which their elders could only have dreamed of. Golfers are fitter, stronger, technically more proficient, and mentally stronger at a younger age now. The roll call of aspiring mega stars is long and

impressive – Sergio Garcia, Justin Rose, Charles Howell III, Ty Tryon, Jonathan Byrd, Ian Poulter, Paul Casey, Luke Donald, Aaron Baddeley, Mike Weir to name just a few. Each of them is starting on the road to great things. Some have got further than others, with 2003 Masters champion Mike Weir leading the way, and who would be brave enough to put a limit on how far they might go in the game of golf. They each have time, and talent, on their side. Temperament will perhaps be the determining factor as to how high they fly.

They and others of their age represent the future of golf at the top level and in that sense, we can safely say the game is definitely in good hands. But what about the equipment that's in the hands of the top players? Could that be damaging the game? You don't need to be a traditionalist to be a little concerned about some issues surrounding golf equipment technology.

The last few decades of the 20th century saw unprecedented developments in the way clubs are built, the materials used, and crucially the way they perform. Shafts have got longer and lighter, clubheads have grown bigger, and the inherent properties of the materials used means the ball comes off the clubface hotter and faster. Miss-hits are no longer punished in the same way as 20 or 30 years ago. A 'necky' strike with a persimmon driver would see the ball take off low and slice weakly to the right. The same strike with an enormous titanium-headed driver produces a shot of such an impressive flight that it is almost indistinguishable, at least to everyone but the player himself, from a pure hit.

As if that were not significant enough, golf ball technology has accelerated at an even faster pace. In real terms, the ball alone is responsible for probably an extra 30 or 40 yards in the average drive of the leading tour professionals over the last decade or so. That is staggering and, like it or not, it accurately reflects just how clever the manufacturers have become. Building clubs and balls isn't an art anymore, it's a science.

Statistics likes this cannot be ignored. It is argued by some people in positions of great authority and knowledge that club and ball technology is in danger of ruining the game as we know it. Some of the top

- ***1*** *Sergio Garcia*
- ***2*** *Charles Howell*
- ***3*** *Ian Poulter*
- ***4*** *Aaron Baddeley*
- ***5*** *Justin Rose*
- ***6*** *Jonathan Byrd*
- ***7*** *Paul Casey*
- ***8*** *Mike Weir*

players have recently admitted this, to the extent that we have witnessed the bizarre scenario in recent years of players expressing concern that the ball is going too far...and they're the ones hitting it that far. It's not their fault, of course. They have a professional interest – and an obligation – to play the best equipment available to them. It's all very well being a traditionalist outside the ropes; just don't expect to see a tour pro sacrificing 30 yards off the tee in order to champion the cause.

But it is a problem that won't go away on its own. And it has massive implications for the game in general, not least in the future of the way golf courses might be designed. Right now at tournaments all over the world, fairway bunkers are being made redundant as pros airmail their drives straight over them.

And it's not just the likes of Tiger Woods, Ernie Els, Phil Mickelson – the big hitters of the game – who are responsible. It's becoming normal for par-5s to be reduced to a driver and mid-iron approach shot. Par-4s are frequently overpowered with a driver, sand-wedge approach. More to the point, a driver isn't even needed half the time. Often, a long-iron tee shot and mid-iron second shot are enough. As a direct result, some of our classic layouts, which are rightly cherished, such as Sunningdale Old Course, have been rendered obsolete – in essence, considered too easy and too short to host a pro tournament.

And holes that were until as recently as the early 1990s thought to be fearsome are being demolished. Remember when Nick Faldo won the 1992 Open Championship at Muirfield? On the par-4 18th he had to nail a driver and a 3-iron, two majestic shots, to secure the precious par he needed for victory. And it wasn't as if there was a gale blowing into his face, just a gentle cross-breeze. That's a world apart from what happened 10 years later when the championship returned to Muirfield and Ernie Els emerged victorious. That week the 18th was being tackled with a big hit with a driver and a little pitch, or just as worryingly a 2- or 3-iron off the tee followed by a simple mid-iron second shot.

If golf club technology is not reined in, at least partially, it will have the almost inevitable, and slightly worrying, knock-on effect of architects resorting to ever-increasing yardages as a golf course's main form of defence. It's happening already. The Old Course at St Andrews had been stretched from 6,900 yards in the late 1970s to a mighty 7,115 yards when Tiger won the Open in 2000. And Augusta National measured 6,905 yards when Seve Ballesteros won the Masters in 1983. When Tiger Woods won it 20 years later, it had gained another 385 yards to reach 7,290. These are more than subtle tweaks.

And still it's probably nowhere near enough. It's been estimated that golf courses today would have to measure somewhere around 8,000 yards in length just to claw back the advantage that new equipment technology has put in the hands of top players in the

• Above
Sunningdale Old Course is now considered too short to hold a men's professional tournament.

last 15 years. Think about that. Imagine adding an extra 100 yards per hole to your home golf course, because on average that's what an 8,000-yard golf course would look like. The figures themselves, while shocking enough, cannot even come close to describing the difficulty the average golfer would experience in playing such a course.

Not so long ago, 7,000-yard golf courses used to be considered monsters. In the 21st century professional game, it's almost entry-level stuff, no more than a minimum requirement. Already, some of the top golf courses which host professional tournaments are creeping up towards the 7,500-yard mark. And this is only the start of the 21st century. These figures do not even begin to take into account the potential implications of another 20 years in the evolution of golf equipment. Or another 50 years. And that is surely what we can expect, for there is no sign whatsoever that any of golf's governing bodies has the inclination, or even the power, to put the technological brakes on in any meaningful way.

Which means the race to produce balls that fly further, and clubs that are even hotter, looks set to continue at speed. There's every likelihood that by the end of this century, tour pros will be competing on golf courses stretched to something like 8,500 yards. This might even be considered normal, unremarkable. Who's to say in the year 2060 there won't be a 9,000-yard golf course hosting a tour event somewhere in the world? And the pros will still hit the par-5s in two!

It could be that golf course design, which has been heading on a dead-straight road for the last couple of hundred years, might now find itself sitting at a T-Junction at the start of the 21st century, at which point it needs to turn in opposite directions to satisfy the needs of both the amateur and professional game. For one thing is certain, you won't get too many average players queuing up to play 8,000-yard golf courses, not unless they have strong masochistic tendencies.

The thing is, in the last 30 years while golf club technology has gone crazy, the average handicap of club golfers has remained static. The equipment gets better, but generally speaking we don't. Not that anyone is especially alarmed by this. Indeed, it's hard to imagine clusters of golfers huddled together in clubhouses all over the world, their brows well-and-truly furrowed as they discuss computer-generated statistical models showing flat-line graphs of average handicap trends.

Fact is, they probably could not give the proverbial monkeys. Nor should they. To the average club golfer the improvement in golf equipment technology manifests itself in harmless, albeit pleasing, results. Golf balls are more durable than they used to be, so don't need replacing as frequently. That saves a few quid, then – excellent news. Do they fly straighter and further? Probably not so anyone would notice. Golf balls are just as easy to lose as they were 20 years ago.

Tour pros might be spinning balls back on the

• Above
Ely Callaway (1919–2001), founder of the world's leading golf club manufacturer.

greens as if tugged on a piece of string, in many cases struggling to contain the backspin that is created by the combination of pure-striking, new-technology golf balls, and super-efficient grooves. But the typical amateur is happy for the ball to simply stop somewhere on the green. Backspin is not even a consideration.

As for the new, hot-faced drivers...well, they sure do make a great sound! Do they make the ball go further? A bit, yes, especially on miss-hits. But not life-changing stuff, certainly nowhere near as dramatic as in the pro game. Generally speaking the benefits to amateurs are probably more psychological than tangible. There's a definite upping of the feel-good factor in hitting a massive-headed titanium driver compared to the dull thwack of a wooden-headed antique from the 1980s.

So maybe we don't have anything to worry about after all. Concerns over equipment technology and whether it's getting out of hand are probably only relevant to the top 0.1 per cent of the golfing population – the leading professionals – which is great news for the game in general. Joe Soap and his mates are not suddenly going to stop playing the classic golf courses, not interested because they no longer represent much of a challenge. Far from it. These courses are plenty tough enough already, not to mention hugely enjoyable, and will remain so for easily another 100 years. Amen to that.

For the average player, the 99.9 per cent of people who play this wonderful game purely for fun, the game doesn't look set to change nearly as much in the next century as it did in the last. Even if the equipment might look different, the essence of the game will remain the same. It will always be engaging, entertaining, uplifting, challenging, and at times utterly infuriating.

None of us would have it any other way.

Greatest Ever Ryder Cup Teams

Chapter TWELVE

12

The European Dream Team

selected by Bernard Gallacher, 1995 Ryder Cup winning captain

Nick Faldo

There was a period in his career – say, between 1988 and 1992 – when Nick Faldo enjoyed the enviable and rare position of being genuinely able to intimidate opponents. Sometimes he didn't even need to hit a shot, or even be on the same fairway. Just the appearance of his name on a leaderboard was more than enough to make some people jump. In matchplay things were much worse, because not only did you have his name and reputation to contend with, and the all the psychological hurdles which that entails, you had the sheer physical presence of the man. At 6ft 4in and 15 stone, shaking your hand and staring right into your eyes...well, intimidating was perhaps not a strong enough word.

No surprise, then, that Faldo's Ryder Cup record is really rather good! He's played more matches, and won more points, than any other golfer in the history of the event. Mentally, Faldo was utterly unshakeable. In moments of the most intense pressure, he was able to come up with the goods – and he did it not just once, but time and time again.

The 1995 Ryder Cup at Oak Hill was typical. Playing the 18th in his singles match against Curtis Strange, he was just under 100 yards from the pin and needing to get down in two to win the Ryder Cup. He knew that. Everyone knew that. And Faldo did exactly what was required, just as he has so many times in major championships, pitching the ball to 4ft and holing the putt. Under pressure, he was the man. As if that were not enough, Faldo's game was relentless in its brilliance. In his prime no other golfer made fewer mistakes.

A hard man? You're not kidding.

• ***Above left***
Nick Faldo playing out of the rough against Curtis Strange in the 1995 Ryder Cup at Oak Hill.

• ***Above right***
Faldo celebrates during the 1993 Ryder Cup at The Belfry.

Seve Ballesteros

That Seve Ballesteros should strike what Jack Nicklaus described as "one of the greatest shots I've ever seen" pretty much sums up this man's impact and influence on the Ryder Cup for Europe. Seve, more than any other person, helped transform these biennial encounters from predictable and one-sided thrashings into the nail-biting, well-matched contests that the Ryder Cup matches became throughout the 1980s and 1990s.

The shot Nicklaus was talking about was a 3-wood, launched from a fairway bunker on to the final green during his singles match against Tom Kite in 1983 at Palm Beach. It only got him a half-a-point, but it was half a point more than any other human being on the planet would have rescued from such an awful spot and it typified the way Seve played the game. You got the feeling that no one hated getting beaten more, so he'd play his heart out to avoid such an awful prospect becoming a reality.

As many Americans discovered first-hand, Seve was a hard man to play against. He wasn't afraid to use a bit of mental gamesmanship, but he never crossed the line. He didn't need to. His game was infused with such genius, and he was able to produce bursts of such sublime play, that he was every bit your classic nightmare opponent. On his own, Seve was the most exciting and charismatic golfer ever to grace the Ryder Cup stage. And his brilliance seemed to rub off on others in the team. When young compatriot Jose Maria Olazabal first played in the Ryder Cup in 1987, the pair of them begun what was to become one of the greatest partnerships in the history of the competition.

Seve is nothing short of a Ryder Cup legend.

• Above
Severiano Ballesteros and Jose Maria Olazabal shaking hands during the 1989 Ryder Cup at the Belfry.

• Inset
Ballesteros and Olazabal checking the line of a putt, Ryder Cup, Muirfield Village, 1987.

Brian Barnes

Brian Barnes was a supremely natural golfing talent, who some say did not even come close to fulfilling his potential. Be that as it may, Barnes knew how to enjoy himself – marking his ball with a beer bottle on one occasion provides a not-so-subtle clue as to his chosen lifestyle habits. He lived his life exactly as he wanted to and you can't say fairer than that. Besides, he won his share of tournaments – 10 in total. So let's forget the underachieving side of his game for a moment and dwell on a single spectacular overachievement, for here is the man who beat Jack Nicklaus twice in one day!

The year was 1975, the venue Laurel Valley in the States. In those days, there were two singles matches in a day. In the morning, Barnes was drawn against Nicklaus, who at that time was the reigning US Masters and USPGA champion – in short, the best player in the world. Barnes was a fine player, but the big Brit was a serious underdog for this encounter. Not that he cared. He went out and gave Nicklaus a thrashing, 4 & 2. At lunchtime, Nicklaus said – jokingly or not, we cannot be sure – that "he's beaten me once, but he won't beat me again". But he did. Barnes went out and gave him another hiding, this time by the margin 2 & 1. Incredible!

Great Britain & Ireland lost this Ryder Cup quite heavily – they often did in the 1960s and 1970s. On the plane home, though, you just hope that amid all the gloom Barnes would have afforded himself the luxury of a little smile of satisfaction.

Neil Coles

Neil Coles looked more like a cuddly professor than a professional sportsman, but he had a golf game that was as brilliant as it was enduring. On paper his Ryder Cup record might not look sensational, but his time coincided with a period of utter and often humiliating US domination. Between 1961 and 1977 when Neil Coles was a member of the GB&I team, the US won seven encounters, lost none, with just a solitary match tied. The points aggregate for those eight years was 146.5 to the United States and just 89.5 to GB&I. As we said, one-sided.

But in that time Coles himself managed to compile a highly respectable record of his own, playing in 40 matches and being unbeaten in 19 of those. In view of the matchplay carnage that was often going on around him – usually at the hands of the likes of Nicklaus, Palmer and Trevino – he did pretty damn well.

But then in any company, Coles was always a class act. His golf swing had, and indeed still has, an almost metronomic rhythm. Whatever club he had in his hands, his swing never missed a beat. Coles didn't have the natural-born physique or the power to bludgeon a ball around a golf course, instead he just caressed it with sweet timing and good technique. He was one of the all-time great fairway wood players, able to place a ball with a precision most other golfers could manage only with the pitching clubs.

If he hadn't suffered such a terrible fear of flying, there's no question that Neil Coles would have been far more famous, successful and wealthy than he ever became.

• Opposite
Brian Barnes playing in the Ryder Cup at Muirfield in 1973.

• Above
Neil Coles at Royal Lytham for the Ryder Cup in 1977.

• Inset
Coles playing the Ryder Cup at Muirfield, Scotland in 1973.

• ***Above left***
European captain celebrates after victory at Muirfield Village in 1987.

• ***Above right***
Jacklin takes a putt as Nicklaus looks on. Royal Birkdale Ryder Cup, 1969.

Tony Jacklin

Think of Tony Jacklin in a Ryder Cup context and two images spring to mind. First is the grainy black-and-white footage of Jack Nicklaus conceding him a 30in putt on the final green in his singles match at Birkdale in 1969. That gave the two of them an honourable half and meant the cup was tied that year. Next, we see him as a smiling Captain Fantastic, leading Europe to stunning victories at the Belfry in 1985 and at Muirfield Village in 1987.

This is all well and good, of course, and there's no question that Jacklin deserves all the credit he gets for helping transform Europe into a team of cashmere-clad, Concorde-flying world-beaters. But it's a shame in some ways that his playing performances aren't given more credence.

He was the linchpin of the GB&I team for seven consecutive cups – during which time he won an Open Championship and a US Open. For a while, he was the best golfer in the world and a force to be reckoned with in any format, the Ryder Cup being no exception. In 35 matches his golf was of a good enough standard for him to be unbeaten 21 times. And bear in mind who he'd have been playing against during that time – the likes of Jack Nicklaus, Tom Watson, Lee Trevino, Johnny Miller, Ray Floyd – basically the US team at the strongest it has ever been in Ryder Cup history.

Jacklin as a player was awesome. It just so happens that as a captain he was even more so. Consequently, that will probably be his enduring legacy.

Colin Montgomerie

Monty's Ryder Cup debut was a classic baptism of fire. The venue was Kiawah Island in 1991, when he was thrust into the first-day foursomes alongside mild-mannered David Gilford against one of America's all-time 'tough nut' pairings – Lanny Wadkins and Hale Irwin, who it is safe to say took no prisoners. As if that were not enough, this Ryder Cup was notorious for tensions running high between the two teams. It got almost too competitive, and the atmosphere got ugly. They called it 'The War on the Shore'. Enough said.

Anyway, they went down 4&2. Monty, big strong chap that he is, must have wondered what on earth had hit him. Just as well he got a rest that afternoon, because he was able to steady himself and come back the next day to win a fourball match and then gain a fighting half against Mark Calcavecchia in the last-day singles. Although the Cup was lost, Monty could hold his head up high.

By the time they went to the Belfry in 1993, Monty was well on his way to becoming Europe's No1 that year – a title he would win for an astonishing seven consecutive years – and he played like it. He has done so ever since, to be frank. The Ryder Cup seems to bring out the best in Monty: not just in his golf, which is at times magnificent, but in his personality. This was seen to good effect in the 2002 Ryder Cup when he led the victorious European team from the front.

• Main picture
Colin Montgomerie playing in the Ryder Cup in 1991 at Kiawah Island.

• **Above**
Sergio Garcia and Jesper Parvenik celebrate during the 1999 Ryder Cup at Brookline.

• **Below**
Garcia celebrating his win at the 2002 Ryder Cup at the Belfry.

Sergio Garcia

The young Spaniard is merely starting out in his Ryder Cup career, a spring chicken compared to every other member of this European dream team. But he deserves his place in the starting line-up because of his record to date, which is excellent, and his undeniable potential to go on to even greater things. There would have to be a very strange and mysterious turn of events for Garcia's name not to be on every Ryder Cup team sheet throughout this decade and long into the next.

He could scarcely have made a more sensational debut. Wearing the European colours for the first time at Brookline in the 1999 contest, Garcia was out in the morning foursomes on the first day partnered with Jesper Parnevik against none other than Tiger Woods and the formidable Tom Lehman. The Spaniard and the Swede were magnificent, winning that match 2 & 1. The pair went out in the afternoon and beat Phil Mickelson and Jim Furyk, then beat Payne Stewart and Justin Leonard the following morning. Three games, three wins. Great stuff!

While Garcia has since had to get used to losing the occasional match, he has established himself as a key member of the team. Upbeat and high-spirited, he lives and breathes the Ryder Cup in the same dramatic fashion that Seve used to in the 1980s and '90s. Motivation, it is safe to assume, is not a problem for Garcia. And he's a great matchplayer, a born winner, as we saw at the 2002 Ryder Cup when he formed a magical partnership with Lee Westwood. Long may it continue!

Bernhard Langer

Bernhard Langer could have been tailor-made for matchplay golf. Utterly inscrutable with a steely look in his eyes, he's been the perfect playing partner – solid, dependable, makes very few unforced errors, and always holds his nerve when the occasion demands it. Not surprisingly, he's probably played with more partners than almost any other Ryder Cupper. You can imagine the team meetings. "B Langer and AN Other; that'll get the job done."

Langer made his debut in 1981 at a time when he had just started to really make his mark (tens of thousands of the cash variety, as it happens) in Europe, winning the previous season's British Masters and having recently finished runner-up to Bill Rogers in the Open Championship at Royal St George's. But he chose a tough year to play his first Ryder Cup, for it was here at Walton Heath that the greatest ever US team in history was assembled. The result was never in doubt, even if the overwhelming one-sided scoreline was a little harsh on the losers, but it gave Langer his first taste of Ryder Cup golf. He liked it so much he came back for a lot more of the same.

Only it wasn't quite the same, because around that time the Europeans got the hang of winning. Langer played a critical role in helping shift the balance of power. In the seven Ryder Cups after his debut, he won many more matches than he lost, a fine achievement given the obvious pedigree of the opposition. It would have been fitting had he holed that infamous putt on the final green against Hale Irwin at Kiawah Island. He certainly deserved to, but as we know it slipped by the hole-side and the Cup that year was lost. Amazingly, Bernhard won the next tournament he played in. That's the character, and class, of the man.

• ***Main picture***
Bernhard Langer collapses after holing out from the bunker during the 1987 Ryder Cup at Muirfield Village.

• Above
Antonio Garrido (left) and Olazabal celebrate during the Ryder Cup at Valderrama, 1997.

Jose Maria Olazabal

Together with Seve Ballesteros, Ollie formed arguably the most successful partnership in the history of the Ryder Cup. His first match was at Muirfield Village in 1987. He'd been a tour professional for only two years, and he was just 21, but his boyish appearance was misleading.

He'd already developed a reputation as a hard-nosed, ferocious competitor and this week would prove to be an overwhelming endorsement of that. Thrust into the heat of battle with his mentor and inspirational countryman, he positively thrived on the pressure, playing the golf of his life and at times appearing to be the stronger of the two playing partners. It was an utterly sensational performance and it helped Europe to their first ever victory on US soil. Ollie's jig of delight on the 18th green during the celebrations later that afternoon is one of the enduring images of that memorable week's golf.

After four Ryder Cup matches his record was fantastic – and he was quite possibly well on his way to compiling one of the most impressive records in the history of the event – but a foot injury sidelined him for two years and he missed the next encounter. When he returned for the 1997 matches in Valderrama, he was soon back into his stride and played a pivotal part in Europe winning the cup. This time Seve was his captain, not his playing partner. But the dynamic duo had struck again. And this time it was on home turf, in Spain. That comeback must have felt very sweet indeed.

Peter Oosterhuis

Until Monty came along and won an incredible seven straight Order of Merit titles, Peter Oosterhuis held what was justifiably considered one of the most impressive records in European golf. Between 1971 and 1974 he was Europe's 'numero uno', the strongest player this side of the Atlantic aside from Tony Jacklin. Looking back, it still is an impressive feat. It's just that it's got a little overlooked since Monty blew it out of the water.

No one overlooked Oosty in his prime, though. For a start, he was 6ft 5in, a height which is usually considered too tall for golf. Not that it held him back. He was a fine player from a young age and having played in the Walker Cup, he straight away turned pro and two years later was playing in the Ryder Cup. He was a seasoned campaigner by the time he partnered Nick Faldo on his debut in 1977, famously winning both their matches on day one. At a combined height of 12ft 9in, they must surely be the tallest partnership in Ryder Cup history!

Strangely, Oosty's game didn't age well. He won his last pro tournament at the tender age of 33, the same year he played in his swansong Ryder Cup. By then he had a better-than-50 per cent record from 28 matches, a fine effort during a lean period for the GB&I team. It's a shame in a way that he wasn't able to stick around a few years longer to be a part of the European glory years.

• Above left
Peter Oosterhuis at Walton Heath for the 1981 Ryder Cup.

• Above right
Oosty playing in the 1977 Ryder Cup at Royal Lytham where he partnered debutant Nick Faldo to two first-day victories.

Christy O'Connor Snr

Tales of Irishman Christy O'Connor Snr are rightly the stuff of legend. He was a colourful character all right, but not even his personality could outshine his skills with a golf club. Christy was a natural-born genius. One of his favourite tricks was to stand on the tee of a medium-length par-3 and hit a ball on to the green with every club in his bag – driver down to wedge. He was that sort of player, possessing such skilful hands that almost nothing was beyond him.

He was a late developer, though. The son of a farmer in County Donegal, it wasn't until he was in his mid-20s that he started to make an impact in the professional game. A fine performance in the 1951 Open seemed to be the launch pad he needed in order to go out and start fulfilling his enormous potential. He duly delivered. In 1955 he claimed a record that will never be taken from him; he won the first ever £1,000 prize offered at a golf tournament in the UK.

That was the year he first stepped into the breach on Ryder Cup duty, by which time he was about to hit 30. He was still playing when the cup went to Muirfield in 1973, which is nothing short of incredible; the man was just coming up to his 50th birthday for heaven's sake. Talent like his doesn't go away overnight. In fact, it never goes away. Even in the late 1990s, he was routinely beating his age in professional senior championships. One of a kind, that's Christy.

• Above
Christy O'Connor Senior playing the Ryder Cup at Royal Birkdale in 1969.

• Inset
O'Connor during the 1973 Ryder Cup at Muirfield.

Ian Woosnam

When Ian Woosnam played in his first Ryder Cup match, the 1983 encounter on American soil at PGA National, one of the things he told his partner Sam Torrance on the first tee was that he felt so nervous he was going to head off into the trees to be sick! Perhaps not the best of signs. But as it happened Woosie came out of his corner fighting and started his round birdie, par, birdie. He never really looked back. That was typical of the man – a class player, a fine competitor, a man with serious bottle. Basically, a good man to have on your side if you knew the going was about to get tough. In Ryder Cups, it usually does.

Woosie played in the next seven Ryder Cup matches and was one of Europe's true stars. He was involved in 31 games, won 14 and halved five. On paper, it might not seem like a particularly strong record, but it is when you take into account the fact that in eight attempts Woosie has never won a last-day singles match. Given everything we know about the man, this is surely one of golf's great unfathomable statistics. No one can offer a plausible explanation, least of all Woosie.

But he still makes it into the European dream team on the basis that his exploits in fourballs and foursomes would almost certainly more than make up for another possible loss in the singles matches.

• Above
Ian Woosnam lifting one from the sand during the 1983 Ryder Cup at the PGA National.

• Inset
Woosie splashes out during the 1993 Ryder Cup at the Belfry.

The United States Dream Team

selected by George Peper

Arnold Palmer

Who else could lead the US dream team other than Arnold Palmer? Some golfers have played more matches, but no other American has won more matches. And it's safe to say, no one did it quite like Arnie. His golf game was a potent cocktail of skill, brute force and bravado that was unparalleled before, or even since, for sheer entertainment value.

But it wasn't just entertaining. His was an awesome and destructive force for any golf course that got in his way. Built like a middleweight boxer, Arnie was not a fan of subtlety. He wanted to beat a golf course to a pulp, his weapons not fists but crushing drives and mighty iron shots, allied to what Jack Nicklaus described as one of the best chip-and-putt short games ever seen. When he was on his game, opponents were knocked over like ninepins, powerless in the face of the unstoppable Arnie charge. His record of 22 wins in 32 matches is justifiably impressive.

Arnie wasn't always invincible, though. Sometimes, he'd get himself into tight spots that even his remarkable powers of recovery could not overcome. In many ways, that was part of the attraction – you never really knew what was coming next. But you knew it would be worth watching. Like Lee Trevino once said, Arnold could attract a bigger gallery to watch him tie his shoelaces than the majority of other golfers might muster with even their best efforts on the golf course. In that one quip, Trevino pretty much hit the nail on the head and summed up the magnitude of this remarkable man's popularity.

• Above
Arnold Palmer playing in the 1961 Ryder Cup at Royal Lytham.

• Inset
Arnie lines up a putt during the Ryder Cup at Muirfield in 1973.

Jack Nicklaus

The way Jack Nicklaus dominated the major championships, and the tournament scene in general, you'd have thought he'd have been invincible in a head-to-head confrontation. No one knew how to bully an opponent, psychologically speaking, better than Jack. The Golden Bear surely only had to prowl on to the first tee and the knees of his opponents would turn to jelly.

But Nicklaus suffered, if you can call it that, in the same way Tiger Woods has in his Ryder Cup career. An 18-hole match is a complete lottery, simply on the basis that anyone who makes a Ryder Cup team can obviously play a bit and can therefore shoot the lights out on any given day. They might not have beaten Jack over four rounds, but in one round...well, anything could happen. And on eight occasions it did; the Golden Bear got whupped.

But hey, let's not get carried away. These things are all relative. Jack Nicklaus is an automatic entry to this all-time Ryder Cup list because his game travelled well and the man himself wasn't fussy about which format he chose to win at. He played 28 matches and won 17 of them, with another three halved. For anyone else, that would be a great record. Because it's Jack, we're surprised it's not better. That's as much a measure of the man's greatness as anything else.

• Picture
What a partnership! Jack Nicklaus and Tom Watson during the Ryder Cup at Walton Heath, 1981.

Billy Casper

Very few golfers – not much more than a handful, in fact – can proudly claim to have played in eight consecutive Ryder Cup encounters. That Billy Casper managed this, compiling one of the most impressive playing records in history, is enough to explain what kind of golfer he was. To justify his selection in the US dream team, we should remind ourselves of his record. He teed up his ball in 37 matches and in 27 of those he was unbeaten. Respect, it's fair to say, is due.

Despite such a notable record in Ryder Cup matches, Casper is probably best known for nailing Arnold Palmer in the 1966 US Open. Eight shots behind tournament leader Arnie with only the back nine to play in the final round, Casper reeled him in like a giant fish on the end of a line. With every sensible drive and smart iron shot, Casper narrowed the gap between himself and the flailing Arnie. Like a fish trying to get away from its would-be captor, the more Arnie tried to attack and thrash his way out of trouble, the worse he made it for himself. Inexplicably, the two were tied when the final round came to its conclusion. Arnie was obviously the weaker of the two for the experience and played poorly the next day to lose the playoff to Casper.

Arnie never did win another major. Casper, on the other hand, went on to add a US Masters title to his name. He won that in a playoff as well. Evidently, head-to-head was his forte.

Lee Trevino

Lee Trevino grew up in poverty, the grandson of a Mexican gravedigger, but nothing was going to stop this extraordinary talent from making a huge name for himself. While his first win was about as big as they come – the 1968 US Open – Trevino took his time making it to the top. For years he worked at a driving range in El Paso, collecting balls for a meagre income which he supplemented – with some considerable success, it must be said – by playing big-money matches against all comers. He famously said that real pressure was playing for 20 bucks when you only had 10 in your back pocket.

Not surprisingly, then, Trevino was a rather useful matchplayer. Those big-money matches had taught him all he needed to know about finishing an opponent off and he applied these skills with ruthless efficiency, but always with a smile and a one-liner. Losing to Trevino was at least never boring. His six consecutive Ryder Cup appearances involved a total of 30 matches and in 23 of those he was not beaten. On paper, it's one of the best records in the Ryder Cup. In reality, it was magical to watch. Trevino had a craft that was individual, but utterly brilliant. He was one of the most gifted ball-strikers of his generation and, considering who was around at the time, that is saying something.

• Opposite
Billy Casper at the 1973 Ryder Cup at Muirfield.

• Above
Lee Trevino in the 1973 Ryder Cup. USA won the event 19–13.

Sam Snead

There are many who say that Sam Snead was the greatest natural talent who ever played the game of golf. Certainly his was the most enduring talent of all. On the main tour, his exploits are rightly still the stuff of legend. At a time when most people are looking forward to collecting their bus pass, Snead was still competing with the world's best golfers. Not just competing, either. When he was 62, he almost won the 1974 USPGA Championship, losing out only to Jack Nicklaus and Lee Trevino, who were half his age and in their prime.

In any kind of matchplay format, Slammin' Sam was awesome. His effortless long driving and classy iron play could simultaneously overwhelm opponents and golf courses. It's just as well for the rest of the world's golfers that his putting wasn't red-hot, otherwise he'd have been unbeatable.

As it was, he was 'only' almost unbeatable. Not surprisingly, in the Ryder Cup he was pretty impressive. He played 13 matches (not many, but then two Ryder Cups he qualified for were cancelled due to the Second World War) and lost only two, which is amazing...primarily for the fact that he should have lost at all.

Can you imagine what the members of the then GB&I team must have been thinking when they stood on the first tee and looked across at the figure of Snead? You'd have to hazard a guess that they weren't overly optimistic. Still, two of them turned him over. Knowing what Snead was like, he'd have been the first to buy his victor a drink at the bar.

Lanny Wadkins

For the best part of two decades, Lanny Wadkins was a stalwart of the US Ryder Cup team. If team selection had been dependent solely on wild cards, rather than the qualification system that existed, you feel sure that Wadkins would have been the first name at the top of any captain's list. To use the technical expression, his selection was a 'total no-brainer'.

Wadkins was like a gunfighter out of some old-fashioned cowboy film – quick on the draw, firing accurate shots as though nothing came more naturally to him. And in Ryder Cup matches, with his heart on one sleeve and the Stars and Stripes on the other, he played as though his life depended on it. He was fiercely competitive and totally focused on winning.

And he had serious bottle – he didn't flinch once, a characteristic that was never more evident than during the final-day single matches at the 1983 Ryder Cup in Palm Beach, Florida. Captain Jack Nicklaus was staring down the barrel of a home defeat on US soil, for the first time in the Cup's history, when up stepped Wadkins the gunslinger to save the day. His wedge shot into the final green, which finished stone dead, is one of the greatest shots in Ryder Cup history – judged not on technical merit, for it was a shot that any golfer could have pulled off, but on sheer guts and nerves of steel. Not many golfers could do that.

He was unbeaten in 22 of his 33 matches. The 11 Brits and Europeans who took Wadkins' scalp could rightly claim to have beaten one of the toughest matchplayers who ever played the game.

• ***Opposite***
Sam Snead at the US Open of 1940.

• ***Above***
Lanny Wadkins playing out of the rough during the Ryder Cup at Kiawah Island, 1991.

Julius Boros

Julius Boros had a golf swing that was smoother than honey being poured from a jar. It was just beautiful to watch – the epitome of poetry in motion. It didn't just look the part, though. This was a swing that got the job done, too. Not only was his game good enough to secure three major championship victories in an era that featured the likes of Jack Nicklaus and Arnold Palmer at the height of their powers, but to this day he remains the oldest person to have won a major championship – clinching the 1968 USPGA Championship at the age of 48 years and four-and-a-bit months. No other winner of a major has come within a couple of years of that landmark. Given the way the game is going in the 21st century, with emphasis on power and youthful athleticism, it could be a record that the Boros name gets to keep forever.

His game lost none of its potency in the switch from strokeplay to matchplay. In four Ryder Cup appearances he played 16 matches and lost only three, which is a strike rate to rival the very best. And keep in mind he was the grand old age of 47 when he played in his last Ryder Cup match for the US. Not many have turned out for their country at that age, and least of all been successful with it.

*• **Above***
Julius Boros didn't turn pro until he was 30 but still played in four Ryder Cups.

Larry Nelson

Serving in the Vietnam War could hardly be described as having its benefits, but it probably puts things in perspective. Larry Nelson did his time in that horrific conflict and after that – maybe not a lot seemed important, certainly not a game of golf, which is perhaps why he seemed utterly impervious to pressure. Even in the biggest tournaments, at the critical time he was able to keep playing his quietly efficient, methodical game while his opponents felt the heat and withered down the home stretch.

Whatever the theories, the fact is Nelson was a tough man to play against. His purple patch lasted only a relatively short period – less than a decade, in fact – but he was sensible enough to use that time fruitfully and win a couple of USPGA Championships and a US Open.

He also made a definite impression on the Ryder Cup and his record of played 13, won nine, and halved one, is strong by any standards. His efforts are perhaps easily overlooked simply because he went about his business in such an unassuming and modest way. Nelson didn't so much overpower a golf course as chip away at its defences. Opponents felt themselves subjected to similar treatment and, all too often, the experience proved painful.

• Above
Larry Nelson at the 1981 Ryder Cup, Walton Heath.

• Below
Nelson after missing a chip during the 1987 Ryder Cup at Muirfield Village.

Walter Hagen

Golf's ultimate showman wasn't averse to a bit of gamesmanship, like walking on to the first tee and saying: "Who's going to finish second, then?" But, as they say, Hagen had the 'go' to go with the 'show'. In fact, the man was virtually unbeatable in head-to-head competition. In the 1920s when the USPGA was a matchplay event, he won it four times in a row, five times in all – which is staggering.

Not surprisingly the Ryder Cup, which was only introduced when Hagen was in his mid-30s and arguably at the end of his prime playing days, suited him down to a tee. In his day, there weren't so many matches played in each Ryder Cup as there are now, so in the five times he played for his country he only had nine games. He won seven of them, though, and halved another, which isn't shabby!

Hagen had what you might call an ungainly swing, with quite a pronounced upper-body sway as he delivered the club to the back of the ball, but he hit it a long way and that was pretty much his objective. Plodding it down the middle would not have suited him at all. Hagen was great in the true sense of the word, a golfer who enjoyed every single minute of his playing career. Whether he was winning (frequently) or losing (rarely) his attitude did not change one iota.

• ***Above***
Walter Hagen in action during a match between England and America, 1920. The match, witnessed by Samuel Ryder, became his inspiration for the Ryder Cup.

• ***Below***
Hagen smiling after winning the Open Golf Championship at Sandwich, 1928.

Hale Irwin

Ah, the mild-mannered, bespectacled Hale Irwin. Looked like a bank clerk, only he got his hands on a lot more money. Before he ditched the glasses and started dominating the US Seniors Tour, Irwin was one of the fiercest matchplay competitors you could ever have the misfortune of running into. A lot of Europeans did, most of them coming off second best.

In his prime Irwin had a quiet way about him. His game wasn't flashy, he didn't have a flamboyant-looking golf swing, nor did he hit the ball out of sight. But he was an accomplished golfer in every department of the game. He drove the ball uncannily straight, kept his rhythm, hit a lot of greens in regulation and putted nicely. More to the point, he had an astute golfing brain. He was able to stay calm under pressure and make very few mental errors, and he produced the shots when he needed to. In short, a nightmare opponent.

Not only did he win back-to-back World Matchplay titles at Wentworth, when the event boasted some real big guns, but he also compiled an impressive Ryder Cup record in consecutive matches between 1975 and 1981. He then came back to Kiawah Island at the age of 46 and carried on much the same – winning two matches and gaining the vital half-point on the last green against Bernhard Langer.

• Above
Hale Irwin and Bernhard Langer head for the final green of the 1991 Ryder Cup at Kiawah Island.

• Inset
Irwin at the Ryder Cup, 1981, Walton Heath.

Tom Kite

Winning majors might have been a problem for Tom Kite – in truth he probably should have more than a solitary US Open to his name – but winning at matchplay most definitely was not. The man was a ruthless slayer of European golfers. In the 1989 singles at the Belfry, he inflicted on poor Howard Clarke one of the heaviest ever defeats in Ryder Cup history – 8&7, thank you very much. And in his last ever Ryder Cup match, again at the Belfry in the singles in 1993, he annihilated Bernhard Langer by the unambiguous margin of 5&3. Two European tough nuts, then, crushed by the quiet man in the glasses.

Kite's golf was a game of two halves. Not a long hitter – in fact, a definite short hitter – he merely used tee shots as a means of getting the ball somewhere near his 'patch' – in other words, inside 100 yards. With a wedge in his hands he was deadly; basically, no one controlled the distance of their pitch shots better than Kite. And he knew how to putt a bit, too.

The worst thing of all for the poor Europeans who went up against him was that the mental frailties which seemed to blight him in the major championships, often resulting in spectacular back-nine collapses, just didn't seem to be a factor in matchplay.

• Above
Tom Kite putts for a par at the Belfry during the 1989 Ryder Cup.

• Opposite
Tiger Woods plays out of a bunker, during the 34th Ryder Cup at the Belfry 2002.

Tiger Woods

Last but not least, the Tiger. Did you really think we were going to leave him out? Okay, so his first few Ryder Cups were strangely unspectacular affairs, during which he lost more matches than he won. But he's just been getting into his stride. He has to be. Let's face it, he was the most successful amateur in history, winning three straight US Amateur titles, which even Bobby Jones couldn't do. You don't achieve something like that without possessing a bit of a knack for matchplay golf. We certainly saw plenty of it in the 2002 Ryder Cup. He was awesome.

But the fact is, if ever the world's best player stood a chance of getting turned over, this is the format to do it. Ryder Cup matches are only 18 holes. Compared to a regular tour event, that's like a mad sprint for the finishing line. Anything can happen. Also, he has a partner for most of the games, which might not be quite Tiger's cup of tea. He's used to beating these guys into the ground week-in, week-out.

Signs are, however, that he's just beginning to get the hang of this Ryder Cup malarkey, which is bad news for Europe. You'd have to predict that he will be playing Ryder Cup golf until at least the year 2016, by which time he'd have played in 10 of these things. Would you seriously bet money that he won't by then be the leading points scorer of all time? Does the Pope ride in a golf buggy? Come on, there isn't a single record that isn't in Tiger's sights. It's just a matter of time.

Who would win?

Fine players through and through on both sides, but the US dream team just gets the nod by virtue of superior firepower right down the order of play. But we reckon it would be close. Call the scoreline 15-13.

Ryder Cup Individual Records

NICK FALDO
1977 / 79 / 81 / 83 / 85 / 87 / 89 / 91
1993 / 95 / 97
Played-46, Won-23, Lost-19, Halved-4

SEVE BALLESTEROS
1979 / 83 / 85 / 87 / 89 / 91 / 93 / 95
Played-37, Won-20, Lost-12, Halved-5

BRIAN BARNES
1969 / 71 / 73 / 75 / 77 / 79
Played-25, Won-10, Lost-14, Halved-1

NEIL COLES
1961 / 63 / 65 / 67 / 69 / 71 / 73 / 77
Played-40, Won-12, Lost-21, Halved-7

TONY JACKLIN
1967 / 69 / 71 / 73 / 75 / 77 / 79
Played-35, Won-13, Lost-14, Halved-8

COLIN MONTGOMERIE
1991 / 93 / 95 / 97 / 99 / 02
Played-28, Won-17, Lost-6, Halved-5

SERGIO GARCIA
1999 / 02
Played-10, Won-6, Lost-3, Halved-1

BERNHARD LANGER
1981 / 83 / 85 / 87 / 89 / 91 / 93 / 95
1997 / 02
Played-42, Won-21, Lost-15, Halved-6

JOSE MARIA OLAZABAL
1987 / 89 / 91 / 93 / 97 / 99
Played-28, Won-15, Lost-8, Halved-5

PETER OOSTERHUIS
1971 / 73 / 75 / 77 / 79 / 81
Played-28, Won-14, Lost-11, Halved-3

CHRISTY O'CONNOR SNR
1955 / 57 / 59 / 61 / 63 / 65 / 67 / 69
1971 / 73
Played-36, Won-11, Lost-21, Halved-4

IAN WOOSNAM
1983 / 85 / 87 / 89 / 91 / 93 / 95 / 97
Played-31, Won-14, Lost-12, Halved-5

ARNOLD PALMER
1961 / 63 / 65 / 67 / 71 / 73
Played-32, Won-22, Lost-8, Halved-2

JACK NICKLAUS
1969 / 71 / 73 / 75 / 77 / 81
Played-28, Won-17, Lost-8, Halved-3

BILLY CASPER
1961 / 63 / 65 / 67 / 69 / 71 / 73 / 75
Played-37, Won-20, Lost-10, Halved-7

LEE TREVINO
1969 / 71 / 73 / 75 / 79 / 81
Played-30, Won-17, Lost-7, Halved-6

SAM SNEAD
1937 / 39 / 41 / 47 / 49 / 51 / 53
1955 / 59
Played-13, Won-10, Lost-2, Halved-1

LANNY WADKINS
1977 / 79 / 83 / 85 / 87 / 89 / 91 / 93
Played-33, Won-20, Lost-11, Halved-2

JULIUS BOROS
1959 / 63 / 65 / 67
Played-16, Won-9, Lost-3, Halved-4

LARRY NELSON
1979 / 81 / 87
Played-13, Won-9, Lost-3, Halved-1

WALTER HAGEN
1927 / 29 / 31 / 33 / 35
Played-9, Won-7, Lost-1, Halved-1

HALE IRWIN
1975 / 77 / 79 / 81 / 91
Played-20, Won-13, Lost-5, Halved-2

TOM KITE
1979 / 81 / 83 / 85 / 87 / 89 / 93
Played-28, Won-15, Lost-9, Halved-4

TIGER WOODS
1997 / 99 / 02
Played-15, Won-5, Lost-8, Halved-2

Index

The pictures in this book
were provided courtesy of the following:

GETTY IMAGES,

101 Bayham Street, London NW1 0AG.

l

HOBBS GOLF COLLECTION,

5 Winston Way, New Ridley, Northumberland NE43 7RF.

l

COLORSPORT

The Courtyard, Lynton Road, London N8 8SL.

l

PHIL SHELDON GOLF PICTURE LIBRARY,

40 Manor Road, Barnet, Hertfordshire EN5 2JQ.

Book design and artwork by Darren Roberts.

Series Editors Jules Gammond and Tim Exell.

Written by Steve Newell.

Edited and Proofed by Alan Pearey and Michael Heatley.

Script Consultant George Peper.